MICROSOFT SHAREPOINT USER GUIDE

The Ultimate Handbook for Storing, Organizing, Sharing and Accessing Information from any Device

MARK O. HERBERT

DISCLAIMER

The contents of this book are provided for informational and entertainment purposes only. The author and publisher make no representations or warranties with respect to the accuracy, applicability, completeness, or suitability of the contents of this book for any purpose.

The information contained within this book is based on the author's personal experiences, research, and opinions, and it is not intended to substitute for professional advice. Readers are encouraged to consult appropriate professionals in the field regarding their individual situations and circumstances.

The author and publisher shall not be liable for any loss, injury, or damage allegedly arising from any information or suggestions contained within this book. Any reliance you place on such information is strictly at your own risk.

Furthermore, the inclusion of any third-party resources, websites, or references does not imply endorsement or responsibility for the content or services provided by these entities.

Readers are encouraged to use their own discretion and judgment in applying any information or recommendations contained within this book to their own lives and situations.

Thank you for reading and understanding this disclaimer.

TABLE OF CONTENTS

CHAPTER ONE
INTRODUCTION TO MICROSOFT SHAREPOINT

Overview of SharePoint

Microsoft SharePoint is a web-based collaborative platform that integrates with Microsoft Office. Launched in 2001, it primarily serves as a document management and storage system, but it is highly configurable and usage varies substantially between organizations. SharePoint is widely used to create websites, manage information, and facilitate team collaboration.

SharePoint offers a range of benefits that can transform how organizations work. Here are some of the key advantages:

- **Enhanced Collaboration and Communication:** SharePoint fosters a collaborative environment by providing central storage for documents, real-time co-authoring capabilities, and integrated communication tools like team chats and discussions. This breaks down information silos and empowers teams to work together more effectively.

- **Streamlined Document Management:** Say goodbye to document chaos! SharePoint offers centralized document libraries with version control, easy access, and permission controls. You can find the latest version of a document quickly, and ensure everyone's working on the right file.

- **Increased Productivity and Efficiency:** By streamlining collaboration and document management, SharePoint frees up valuable time and reduces wasted effort. Employees can locate information faster, stay on the same page with projects, and automate tasks, leading to a significant boost in productivity.

- **Improved Access and Mobility:** Accessibility is a major benefit. SharePoint allows users to access documents and team sites from anywhere, anytime, using a web browser or mobile app. This keeps everyone connected and in sync, even when working remotely.

- **Enhanced Security and Compliance:** SharePoint takes security seriously. It offers granular permission controls to ensure only authorized users can access sensitive information. Additionally, features like data encryption and auditing help organizations meet compliance requirements.

- **Customization and Extensibility:** SharePoint is flexible and adaptable. It allows for customization through features like custom lists, workflows, and web parts. Additionally, Microsoft offers a robust development platform for extending SharePoint's functionality with custom applications.

- **Integration with Microsoft 365:** A major benefit for Microsoft 365 users is the seamless integration between SharePoint and other applications like Teams, OneDrive, and Power BI. This creates a unified environment where you can work with data and collaborate effortlessly across different tools.

- **Scalability and Enterprise-grade Capabilities:** SharePoint can handle the demands of businesses of all sizes. It scales to accommodate growing data volumes and user bases, making it a reliable solution for both small teams and large enterprises.

In summary, SharePoint empowers businesses to streamline collaboration, boost productivity, ensure information security, and work smarter overall.

History and Evolution

SharePoint's story starts back in the early 2000s, during the development of Microsoft Office XP. It wasn't a single idea, but rather the merging of two projects:

- **Office Server:** This project, with roots in FrontPage and Office Server Extensions, aimed to make collaboration easier by providing "Team Pages" for simple, bottom-up teamwork.

- **Tahoe:** This project focused on creating top-down portals, search functionalities, and document management features.

These projects combined to form the first iteration known as **SharePoint Portal Server 2001**.

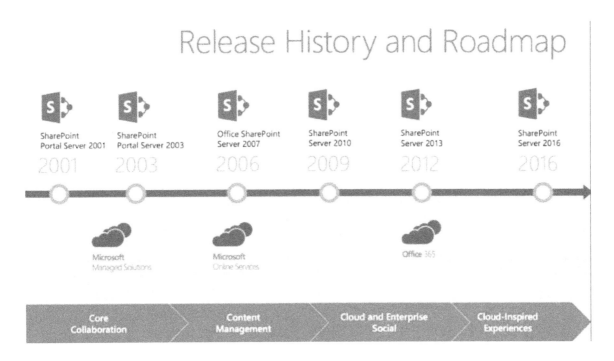

Here are some key milestones in SharePoint's evolution:

- **2007: SharePoint 2007** marked a significant leap by integrating with Microsoft Exchange for Public Folders and connecting its front-end to Office applications. This expanded SharePoint's capabilities as a business platform.

- **2010: SharePoint 2010** brought improvements in user experience, including drag-and-drop functionality and social features like "Follow" and "Share" buttons.

- **2013: SharePoint 2013** offered better mobile access and a more cloud-oriented approach.

- **The Cloud Era:** The introduction of **SharePoint Online** as part of Microsoft 365 subscriptions was a game changer. Cloud deployment made it easier to set up and manage, reaching a wider audience.

- **Modern Era:** Recent versions (2016 & 2019) continue to refine the user experience and integrate seamlessly with other Microsoft 365 tools like Teams.

The Rise of Teams: While SharePoint remains the foundation for document management and collaboration, Microsoft Teams has emerged as a more user-friendly face for accessing and interacting with SharePoint content. This integration showcases SharePoint's adaptability and its role as the backbone for a wider collaborative ecosystem.

SharePoint in the Microsoft Ecosystem

SharePoint plays a central role within the Microsoft ecosystem, acting as a strong foundation for collaboration and content management. Here's how it integrates with other key Microsoft products:

- **Microsoft 365:** SharePoint is a core component of Microsoft 365 subscriptions. This tight integration allows users to seamlessly access and work on SharePoint documents within familiar applications like Word, Excel, and PowerPoint.

- **Microsoft Teams:** While Teams offers a chat-based collaboration experience, it heavily relies on SharePoint in the background. Team files and folders are actually stored in SharePoint, making them accessible and manageable through both Teams and the SharePoint interface.

- **OneDrive:** SharePoint and OneDrive work together to provide personal and team cloud storage. Individual users can leverage OneDrive for personal files, while SharePoint offers team-based storage and collaboration features.

- **Power BI:** SharePoint can serve as a data source for Power BI, allowing users to create insightful reports and dashboards from information stored within SharePoint lists and libraries.

- **Azure:** For organizations with complex data needs, SharePoint can integrate with Microsoft Azure services for advanced data storage, analytics, and backup functionalities.

Benefits of this Ecosystem Integration:

This tight integration within the Microsoft ecosystem offers several advantages:

- **Unified User Experience:** Users can work seamlessly across different applications without worrying about data silos or switching between platforms.

- **Enhanced Collaboration:** Information sharing and collaboration become effortless as documents and data flow freely between connected tools.

- **Improved Productivity:** Streamlined workflows and centralized access to information boost overall team productivity.

Beyond Integration:

- **Microsoft Graph:** The Microsoft Graph acts as a central nervous system for the Microsoft ecosystem, allowing applications like SharePoint to interact and share data with each other.

- **Active Directory:** SharePoint leverages Active Directory for user authentication and authorization, ensuring consistent access control across different applications.

By integrating with these various Microsoft products and services, SharePoint becomes a cornerstone for a comprehensive and collaborative work environment.

CHAPTER TWO
GETTING STARTED WITH SHAREPOINT

Setting Up SharePoint

There are two main ways to set up SharePoint, depending on which version you'll be using: SharePoint Online (cloud-based) or SharePoint Server (on-premises). Here's a basic overview for each:

SharePoint Online (Microsoft 365):

- **Prerequisites:** You'll need a Microsoft 365 subscription that includes SharePoint Online (like Business Essentials, Microsoft 365 Business Standard, or a higher tier plan).

- **Setup Process:** Generally simpler. Signing up for a Microsoft 365 plan automatically provisions SharePoint Online for your organization.

- **Here's a simplified rundown:**

  1. **Sign in:** Access the Microsoft 365 admin centre using your admin credentials.

  2. **Create a site:** Locate the "SharePoint" section and choose "Create site."

  3. **Select your site type:** Pick "Team site" for collaboration or "Communication site" for information sharing.

  4. **Configure settings:** Provide a name and description for your site, choose privacy settings (private or public), and add team members.

  5. **Start collaborating:** Once created, your SharePoint site is ready for uploading documents, creating lists, and collaborating with your team.

SharePoint Server (on-premises):

- **Prerequisites:** Requires installing and configuring SharePoint Server software on your organization's servers. This involves more technical expertise.

- **Setup Process:** More complex and involves IT specialists. Here's a general idea:

  1. **Hardware and software setup:** Prepare servers that meet SharePoint Server system requirements and install the software.

  2. **Configuration:** Configure user accounts, permissions, security settings, and features according to your organization's needs.

  3. **Site creation:** Similar to SharePoint Online, authorized users can create team or communication sites.

Additional Resources:

While this is a simplified overview, there are many resources available to help you set up SharePoint effectively. Here are some suggestions:

- **Microsoft's official documentation:** Microsoft provides comprehensive documentation for both SharePoint Online and SharePoint Server, including step-by-step guides for setup, configuration, and management.

- **Online tutorials and videos:** Numerous websites and channels offer video tutorials and guides on setting up and using SharePoint. These can be a helpful resource for visual learners.

Remember, the best approach depends on your specific needs and technical expertise. If you're unsure, starting with SharePoint Online as part of a Microsoft 365 subscription might be a simpler option.

Accessing SharePoint

Accessing SharePoint depends on whether you're using SharePoint Online (cloud-based) or SharePoint Server (on-premises). Here's a breakdown for both:

SharePoint Online (Microsoft 365):

- **Web browser:** This is the primary method for accessing SharePoint Online. Open a web browser and navigate to site.

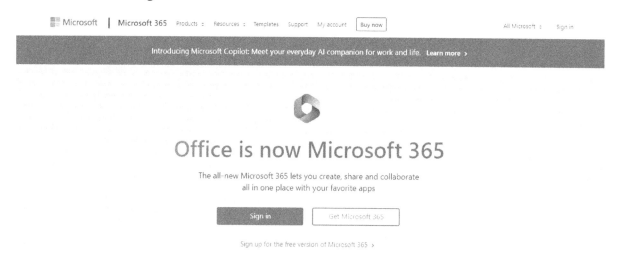

- **Login credentials:** Sign in using your Microsoft 365 work or school account email address and password.

- **App launcher:** Once logged in, look for the app launcher icon (usually a grid of squares) in the top left corner.
- **Locate SharePoint:** Click the app launcher and then select "SharePoint" from the list of applications.

SharePoint Server (on-premises):

- **Internal company URL:** In this scenario, your organization's IT department will provide you with the specific internal URL to access your SharePoint Server site.
- **Login credentials:** Use your organization's login credentials to access the SharePoint Server site.

By following these steps and considering the additional tips, you should be able to access your SharePoint environment and start collaborating with your team.

Basic Navigation

Navigating SharePoint can be intuitive, especially in the modern SharePoint experience. Here's a rundown of the essentials:

Layout:

- **Navigation bar (left-hand side):** This vertical pane provides the main navigation for your SharePoint site. It typically contains links to:
    - **Home:** This brings you back to the landing page of your SharePoint site.
    - **Content libraries:** Lists document libraries where you can store and manage various files.

- o **Lists:** Links to custom lists used to organize specific information.

- o **Team sites or communication sites:** If your SharePoint is connected to a hub site, you might see links to other relevant team or communication sites.

- o **Additional links:** Depending on your site's setup, you might see custom links added for specific purposes.

- **Title bar (top):** This section displays the name and logo of your SharePoint site. Clicking the logo typically takes you back to the home page.

- **Search bar (top):** Use this bar to search for documents, people, or specific content within your SharePoint site.

- **Suite bar (top right):** This bar offers quick access to your Microsoft 365 profile, settings, notifications, and the app launcher (grid icon) where you can find other Microsoft 365 applications.

Navigating with the Navigation Bar:

- Click on any link in the navigation bar to access the corresponding content library, list, team site, or other linked page.

- Some links might have dropdown menus revealing subfolders or additional options within that section.

Additional Navigation Tips:

- **Breadcrumbs:** Many pages within SharePoint display breadcrumbs at the top, indicating your current location within the site hierarchy. You can click on previous sections in the breadcrumbs to navigate back.

- **Search functionality:** The search bar is a powerful tool for finding specific information or files quickly.

By understanding this basic layout and using the navigation bar effectively, you should be able to find your way around most SharePoint sites. Remember, the specific navigation elements might vary slightly depending on your organization's setup and customizations.

SharePoint Editions and Pricing

SharePoint comes in two main flavours: SharePoint Online (cloud-based) and SharePoint Server (on-premises). Their pricing structures differ significantly:

SharePoint Online:

- **Subscription-based model:** You access SharePoint Online as part of a Microsoft 365 subscription. There are various plans available, each catering to different needs and offering a set of included features.

- **Two main plans for SharePoint Online:**

  - **SharePoint Online Plan 1:** This plan starts around $5 per user per month and is suitable for small businesses or teams that need basic document management and collaboration features.

  - **SharePoint Online Plan 2:** This plan costs around $10 per user per month and offers more advanced features like advanced search, eDiscovery, and unlimited storage. It's ideal for larger organizations with complex collaboration needs.

- **Additional options:** SharePoint Online can also be included in some higher-tier Microsoft 365 plans (like Office 365 E3 and E5) that offer a broader suite of applications and services.

Here's a tip: It's always best to check the latest pricing information directly from Microsoft's website, as prices can change occasionally. You can find details and comparisons on the official Microsoft 365 SharePoint plans page:

SharePoint Server:

- **Per-server licensing:** This model involves purchasing licenses for the SharePoint Server software itself, which you install on your own servers. There are different editions with varying feature sets, and the cost depends on the chosen edition and the number of server licenses required.

- **More complex pricing structure:** Compared to SharePoint Online, on-premises SharePoint Server has a more intricate pricing structure with factors like Server CALs (Client Access Licenses) and core licenses influencing the overall cost.

Additional considerations for SharePoint Server:

- **On-going maintenance:** Remember, with SharePoint Server, your organization is responsible for managing the hardware, software, security, and ongoing maintenance of the servers.

Choosing the right edition:

The best option for you depends on your specific needs and resources. Here's a quick comparison to help you decide:

- **Choose SharePoint Online if:** You prefer a cloud-based solution with a predictable monthly subscription cost, ease of use, and automatic updates.

- **Consider SharePoint Server if:** You have strict data security requirements, require extensive customization options, or have a large existing infrastructure investment in on-premises servers.

It's wise to carefully evaluate your requirements and potentially consult with an IT professional before making a decision.

CHAPTER THREE
SHAREPOINT ARCHITECTURE

Site Collections and Sites

In SharePoint, understanding the difference between **site collections** and **sites** is crucial for organizing your content and managing permissions effectively.

Site Collection:

- Imagine a site collection as a container. It's the highest level of organization within a SharePoint web application.

- It can hold one or more subsites, all sharing the same:

    - **Owner:** A single administrator oversees the entire site collection.

    - **Permissions:** Permission settings are applied at the site collection level, governing access for all sites within it.

    - **Configuration:** The site collection inherits its configuration (like language, time zone) from the web application.

    - **Content database:** All sites in a collection reside within a single content database.

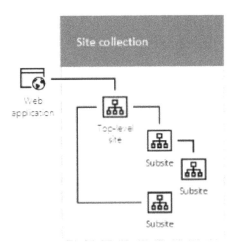

Analogy: Think of a site collection like a ring binder. It holds the binder itself (the top-level site) and any dividers or subfolders (subsites) you add within it. Everything in the binder shares the same overall structure and labelling system.

Sites:

- **Individual websites:** Sites are the building blocks within a site collection. They represent specific departments, projects, or purposes.

- **Subsites:** These are sites created underneath the top-level site within a site collection. They inherit permissions and configuration from the parent site collection but can have unique features or branding.

- **Example:** A company might have a site collection for its Marketing department. This could contain a top-level site for general marketing resources and separate subsites for specific campaigns or teams (e.g., Social Media Marketing site, Content Marketing site).

Benefits of Site Collections:

- **Organized structure:** Site collections help maintain a logical structure for your SharePoint content, grouping related sites together.

- **Efficient permission management:** Managing permissions at the site collection level simplifies administration for similar access needs across multiple sites.

- **Scalability:** You can add more subsites to a site collection as your needs grow, without creating entirely separate entities.

Here are some additional points to remember:

- A single site cannot exist outside of a site collection.

- There are limitations on the number of subsites you can create within a single site collection.

- While subsites inherit some settings from the site collection, they can have some unique configurations, like a different site theme.

By understanding this hierarchical structure, you can effectively organize your SharePoint environment, ensure proper access control, and streamline collaboration within your teams.

Libraries and Lists

SharePoint offers two core content management tools: Libraries and Lists. While they both store information, they have distinct purposes and functionalities:

Document Libraries:

- **Designed for:** Storing, organizing, managing, and sharing files of various types (documents, images, PDFs, etc.).

- **Think of it as:** A digital filing cabinet for your team's essential documents.

- **Key features:**

- **Version control:** Tracks changes made to documents over time, allowing you to revert to previous versions if needed.

- **Metadata and tagging:** Lets you categorize documents with keywords, making them easier to search and filter.

- **Check-in/check-out:** Enables controlled editing to prevent multiple users from modifying a document simultaneously.

- **Workflows:** Automates tasks associated with documents, such as routing approvals or sending notifications.

∨ In site library

	Name ∨	Modified ∨	Modified By ∨
	Employee Onboarding	A few seconds ago	Gregory Zelfond
	General	August 19, 2019	Gregory Zelfond
	Invoices	8 minutes ago	Gregory Zelfond
	Budget.xlsx	April 27	Gregory Zelfond

Lists:

- **Designed for:** Organizing and managing structured data in a tabular format, similar to spreadsheets.

- **Think of it as:** A customizable database for tracking information relevant to your team or project.

- **Key features:**

  - **Rows and columns:** Data is organized in rows (items) and columns (fields) that define the type of information each entry holds (text, numbers, dates, etc.).

  - **Views:** Create different views of the list data to filter and display information based on specific criteria.

  - **Calculated columns:** Automatically generate new data points based on formulas using existing list data.

  - **Conditional formatting:** Apply visual formatting rules to highlight specific entries or trends within the list.

Projects ★

○	Project Name ∨	Link to Site ∨	Client ∨	Project Manager ∨	Status ∨
	SharePoint Migration	Link	Google	Gregory Zelfond	Active
	Office Move	Link	Facebook	John Smith	Closed
	Server Upgrade	Link	Microsoft	John Smith	Closed

Choosing Between Libraries and Lists:

- Use a **document library** when you need to store and collaborate on various file types.

- Use a **list** when you need to track and manage structured data points relevant to your work.

Here's an analogy to illustrate the difference:

- Imagine a library houses books (documents) with different genres (file types). You can categorize them by topic (metadata) and track checkouts (version control).

- Now imagine a list in a library, like a catalogue for those books. It would have columns for Title (text), Author (text), Genre (choice), and Publication Date (date). You can filter this list to find specific books (views) and create calculations like "Books published after 2020" (calculated columns).

By understanding these core functionalities, you can effectively choose between libraries and lists to organize your information within SharePoint and optimize your team's collaboration.

Pages and Web Parts

SharePoint pages and web parts work together to create the visual elements and functionalities you see within your SharePoint sites.

Pages:

- **Think of them as:** The building blocks that define the layout and structure of your SharePoint site. A site can have multiple pages, each serving a specific purpose.

- **Examples of pages:** You can create a team homepage to welcome members, a project page to collaborate on tasks, or a news page to share announcements.

- **Customizable layouts:** Modern SharePoint offers a variety of pre-designed layouts with sections and columns that you can arrange to suit your needs. You can also add custom layouts with more flexibility.

Web Parts:

- **Imagine them as:** Modular components that you add to a SharePoint page to display specific content or functionalities. Think of them like Lego bricks for building your page.

- **Wide variety:** SharePoint offers a vast library of web parts for different purposes. Here are a few examples:

    o **Document libraries web part:** Displays a list of documents from a connected document library.

    o **List web part:** Shows data from a connected SharePoint list.

    o **Calendar web part:** Displays an interactive calendar for team events.

    o **Content embed web part:** Allows embedding external content like videos or web pages.

- **Customization:** Many web parts are configurable, allowing you to adjust their appearance and behaviour to match your needs.

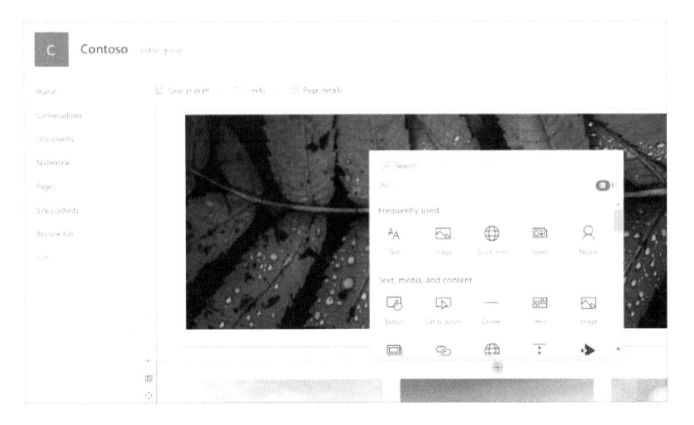

How Pages and Web Parts Work Together:

1. **Create a page:** You start by creating a new page within your SharePoint site.

2. **Choose a layout:** Select a pre-designed layout or create a custom one with sections and columns.

3. **Add web parts:** From the web part toolbox, drag and drop the desired web parts into the designated sections of your page layout.

4. **Configure web parts:** Customize the settings of each web part to determine what content it displays and how it functions.

5. **Publish the page:** Once you're satisfied with the layout and web part configuration, publish the page to make it visible to authorized users.

Benefits of Using Pages and Web Parts:

- **Flexibility:** The combination of pages and web parts allows you to create dynamic and informative SharePoint sites tailored to your specific needs.

- **No coding required:** You don't need coding expertise to build effective SharePoint pages. The drag-and-drop functionality and pre-configured web parts make it user-friendly.

- **Easy updates:** Content updates are straightforward. You can modify web part properties or directly edit the content within the page itself.

By understanding how pages and web parts work together, you can create user-friendly and informative SharePoint sites that enhance collaboration and communication within your teams.

SharePoint Workflows

In SharePoint, workflows automate repetitive tasks and streamline specific business processes. Imagine them as a series of pre-defined instructions that execute automatically based on certain triggers or events.

Here's a breakdown of the key concepts:

- **Think of them as:** Automated mini-programs that execute actions within your SharePoint site.

- **Benefits:** Workflows can save time, improve efficiency, and ensure consistency in how tasks are completed. They can also reduce manual errors and keep team members informed about progress.

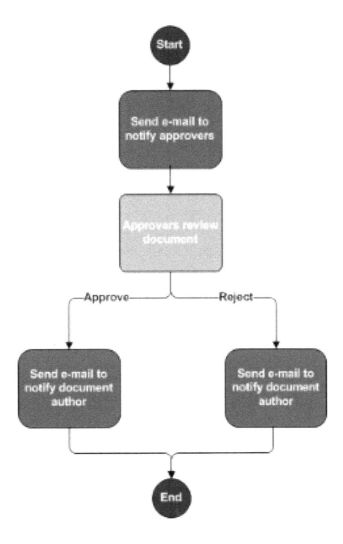

Types of SharePoint Workflows:

- **Approval workflows:** These are common workflows used to route documents or requests for approval through a designated sequence of people.

- **Collection workflows:** These workflows gather information from users, like collecting feedback on a document or survey responses.

- **Status workflows:** These workflows automatically update the status of an item in a list or library based on predefined conditions. For example, a workflow might automatically change the status of a project task from "In Progress" to "Completed" when a certain milestone is achieved.

- **Notification workflows:** These workflows send automatic emails or alerts to designated users based on specific events. For instance, a notification workflow might send an email to a team member when a new document is uploaded to a specific library.

24

How Workflows Function:

1. **Triggers:** A workflow is initiated by a specific event, such as creating a new item in a list, uploading a document to a library, or modifying an existing item.

2. **Actions:** Once triggered, the workflow performs a set of pre-defined actions. These actions can involve:

   - Assigning tasks to specific users.
   - Sending email notifications.
   - Updating the status of an item.
   - Moving or copying items between lists or libraries.
   - Starting other workflows.

3. **Conditions (optional):** Some workflows incorporate conditional logic. Based on specific criteria being met, the workflow might follow different paths or execute different actions.

Creating Workflows:

- **SharePoint Designer (older versions):** In older SharePoint versions, a standalone application called SharePoint Designer was used to create complex workflows.

- **Power Automate (modern SharePoint):** Modern SharePoint leverages Microsoft Power Automate, a web-based tool, for creating workflows. Power Automate offers a user-friendly interface with pre-built templates and connectors for various actions.

Here are some additional points to consider about SharePoint workflows:

- Workflows can significantly enhance the functionality of your SharePoint site, but planning and testing are crucial to ensure they operate as intended.

- The complexity of workflows can vary depending on your needs. Simpler workflows can be created directly within SharePoint, while more intricate automations might require Power Automate.

- Security considerations are important. It's essential to define who can create and edit workflows to maintain control over your SharePoint environment.

By effectively utilizing SharePoint workflows, you can automate manual tasks, streamline processes, and boost overall team productivity.

CHAPTER FOUR
SHAREPOINT FEATURES AND FUNCTIONALITY

Document Management

SharePoint shines as a document management system, offering a centralized location for storing, organizing, collaborating on, and securing your documents. Here's how it streamlines document lifecycles:

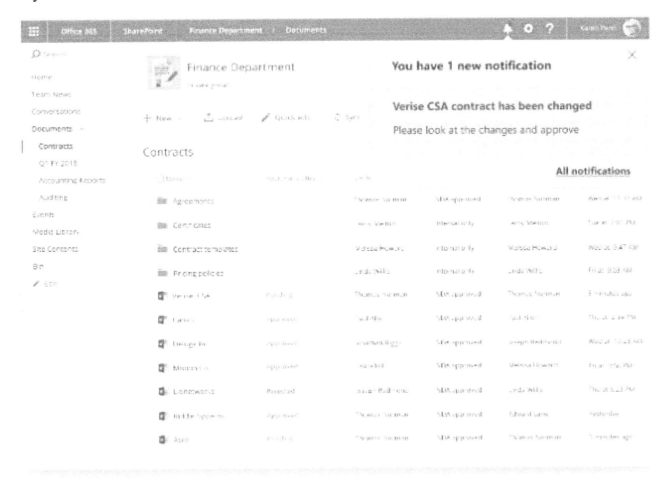

- **Centralized Storage:** Say goodbye to scattered documents across individual computers or network drives. SharePoint provides a single repository for all your documents, making them accessible from anywhere, anytime, and on any device.

- **Version Control:** No more document chaos! SharePoint keeps track of every change made to a document, allowing you to revert to previous versions if needed. This ensures everyone works on the latest version and eliminates confusion.

- **Metadata and Tagging:** Organize your documents efficiently. Add keywords and descriptive tags to categorize documents, making them easier to find through advanced search functionalities.

- **Check-In/Check-Out:** Prevent simultaneous editing conflicts. The check-in/check-out feature ensures only one person edits a document at a time, maintaining data integrity and avoiding accidental overwrites.

- **Security and Permissions:** SharePoint provides granular control over document access. You can assign different permission levels to users and groups, ensuring only authorized users can view, edit, or share documents.

- **Collaboration Features:** SharePoint fosters teamwork on documents. You can co-author documents in real-time, leave comments and suggestions, and share feedback within the platform.

- **Workflows:** Automate repetitive tasks associated with documents. For instance, create workflows to route documents for approval, send notifications upon modification, or manage document lifespans (archiving or deletion).

- **Integration with Microsoft 365:** SharePoint seamlessly integrates with other Microsoft 365 applications like Word, Excel, and OneDrive. This allows for effortless document editing within familiar tools and easy access to the latest versions stored in SharePoint.

Benefits of Using SharePoint for Document Management:

- **Improved Efficiency:** Centralized storage, version control, and search features help users locate documents faster and reduce wasted time.

- **Enhanced Collaboration:** Real-time co-authoring, commenting, and workflow automation streamline teamwork on documents.

- **Increased Productivity:** By simplifying document management processes, SharePoint frees up valuable time for employees to focus on core tasks.

- **Robust Security:** Granular permission controls and access management ensure your confidential documents are protected.

- **Scalability:** SharePoint can accommodate growing document volumes and user bases, making it suitable for businesses of all sizes.

By leveraging SharePoint's document management capabilities, you can establish a well-organized and secure system for handling your organization's critical documents. This leads to better collaboration, increased efficiency, and overall improved information management.

Content Management

SharePoint extends beyond just document management and functions as a comprehensive content management system (CMS). Here's how it caters to various content needs:

SHAREPOINT DMS INTEGRATIONS

ERP

Financial, production, procurement, legal documents, and more

Paper documents · SHAREPOINT DMS · Learning materials

OCR · LMS

Electronic signature

E-SIGNATURE SOFTWARE

- **Document Management:** As discussed earlier, SharePoint excels at storing, organizing, and managing documents. But it also handles other file types:
    - Spreadsheets and presentations
    - Images, audio, and video files
    - Digital assets like logos and branding materials

- **Web Content Management (WCM):** Create and publish web content like news articles, announcements, or team updates directly within SharePoint. It offers:
    - User-friendly editing tools for building web pages with minimal technical expertise.
    - Pre-designed templates and layouts for a consistent look and feel across your site.
    - Approval workflows to ensure content accuracy and maintain brand guidelines.

- **Content Types:** Define reusable templates for specific content types. This ensures consistency and simplifies content creation. For example, a "News Article" content type might include pre-defined fields for title, author, date, and category.

- **Content Search:** SharePoint's powerful search functionality helps users find the information they need quickly. Search can encompass various content types, including documents, web pages, list items, and metadata.

- **Content Approval Workflows:** Automate the review and approval process for different content types. This streamlines content publishing and ensures adherence to quality standards.

- **Integration with External Systems:** SharePoint can connect with external data sources and content repositories, allowing you to manage information from various systems within a central location.

- **Version Control and Rollback:** Similar to documents, SharePoint maintains version history for all content types. This allows you to revert to previous versions if needed or roll back any accidental changes.

Benefits of SharePoint for Content Management:

- **Centralized Content Repository:** A single source of truth for all your organization's content, improving information accessibility and reducing redundancy.

- **Streamlined Content Creation:** User-friendly tools and templates make content creation efficient, even for non-technical users.

- **Content Governance:** Approval workflows and permission controls ensure content quality and adherence to brand guidelines.

- **Improved Findability:** Robust search functionalities help users locate the information they need quickly.

- **Flexibility:** SharePoint can accommodate various content types, making it a versatile CMS solution.

By using SharePoint for content management, you gain a centralized platform to store, organize, publish, and manage all your information assets. This fosters better collaboration, simplifies content governance, and ensures information findability for your team.

Collaboration Tools

SharePoint offers a rich set of tools specifically designed to enhance teamwork and collaboration within your organization. Here are some of the key features that make SharePoint a powerful collaboration platform:

- **Centralized Document Storage and Management:** SharePoint eliminates scattered documents and provides a single source of truth for all your team's files. This ensures everyone has access to the latest versions and reduces confusion.

- **Real-time Co-authoring:** Multiple users can work on the same document simultaneously, fostering efficient collaboration and expediting project completion. Imagine a team working on a proposal together, seeing each other's edits in real-time within the SharePoint interface.

- **Version Control and History Tracking:** No more worries about overwritten content. Version control keeps track of changes made to documents, allowing you to revert to previous versions if needed. Additionally, history tracking provides transparency into who made edits and when.

- **Communication Tools:** SharePoint integrates seamlessly with Microsoft Teams, enabling threaded conversations, document sharing, and task assignments directly within Teams. You can also leverage built-in comments and mentions features within SharePoint itself to facilitate discussions and keep everyone informed.

- **Shared Calendars and Task Lists:** Create and manage team calendars to schedule meetings and track deadlines. Shared task lists help assign tasks, monitor progress, and ensure everyone's on the same page regarding project deliverables.

- **Meeting Integration:** Connect SharePoint with Outlook calendars for easy scheduling and centralized access to meeting agendas and documents.

- **Workflows for Automation:** Automate repetitive tasks associated with collaboration. For instance, create workflows to route documents for approval, send notifications upon task completion, or trigger reminders for upcoming deadlines.

- **Search Functionality:** Find information quickly and easily. SharePoint's robust search capabilities allow users to locate relevant documents, people, or conversations across the platform.

- **Accessibility and Mobility:** Access and collaborate on projects from anywhere, anytime, and on any device. SharePoint offers web browser access and mobile apps for iOS and Android, ensuring flexibility for your team.

Anywhere access to files with OneDrive
Document collaboration with Office apps
Shared content in Teams and Outlook
Intranet sites with Yammer and Stream
Business process with PowerApps & Flow

SharePoint

 Security   AI   Extensibility

Benefits of Using SharePoint Collaboration Tools:

- **Improved Communication and Collaboration:** Centralized document storage, real-time co-authoring, and integrated communication tools streamline teamwork and information sharing.

- **Enhanced Project Management:** Shared calendars, task lists, and workflows keep projects organized, on track, and deadlines met.

- **Increased Productivity:** Automation, centralized access, and improved communication empower teams to work more efficiently.

- **Transparency and Visibility:** Version control, history tracking, and task management features provide clear visibility into project progress for all team members.

- **Mobile Collaboration:** The ability to access and work on projects from mobile devices fosters flexibility and keeps everyone connected.

By leveraging SharePoint's collaboration tools, you can empower your team to work together seamlessly, improve project management, and achieve better results. SharePoint acts as a central hub for communication, document sharing, and task management, fostering a collaborative work environment for your organization.

Search and Discovery

SharePoint offers powerful search and discovery functionalities to help users find the information they need quickly and efficiently within the vast amount of content stored on the platform. Here's a breakdown of its key features:

- **Comprehensive Search:** Search across various content types, including documents, web pages, list items, metadata, and even conversations within Teams chats (if integrated).

- **Refiners and Filters:** Narrow down search results using refiners and filters based on specific criteria like document author, content type, date modified, or custom metadata tags. Imagine searching for all marketing reports created in the last quarter by a specific team member.

- **Search Ranking:** SharePoint prioritizes search results based on relevance. Frequently accessed documents, user activity patterns, and content popularity all influence the ranking to deliver the most relevant information at the top.

- **Keyword Stemming:** Search understands synonyms and variations of keywords, ensuring you find the information you need even if you don't use the exact phrasing. For instance, searching for "marketing plans" might also return results related to "marketing strategies" or "campaign proposals."

- **Search Alerts:** Stay updated on relevant information. Set up search alerts to receive notifications whenever new content matching your search criteria is added to SharePoint.

- **Discovery Features:** Beyond basic search, SharePoint incorporates intelligent features to surface potentially useful content even if users don't explicitly search for it. This can include:

  - **Trending Documents:** Highlighting documents that are being frequently accessed or modified by other users.

  - **Suggested Sites:** Recommending sites or content based on a user's past activity and work patterns.

  - **Promoted Results:** Administrators can promote specific content to ensure it appears prominently in search results for better visibility.

Benefits of SharePoint Search and Discovery:

- **Improved User Experience:** Users can locate the information they need quickly and easily, reducing wasted time spent searching through folders or emails.

- **Enhanced Knowledge Sharing:** Discovery features help users find relevant content they might not have been aware of, fostering knowledge sharing and better utilization of information within the organization.

- **Increased Productivity:** By streamlining information access, users can focus on core tasks instead of getting lost in endless searches.

- **Reduced Information Overload:** The ability to filter and refine searches helps users cut through the clutter and find the specific information they need.

- **Personalized Experience:** Search functionality can be tailored to individual users based on their activity and work context, leading to a more personalized discovery experience.

By using SharePoint's search and discovery features effectively, you can empower your users to find the information they need quickly and make data-driven decisions, ultimately boosting overall productivity and knowledge sharing within your organization.

Security and Compliance

Security and compliance are paramount concerns for any organization managing sensitive data. SharePoint offers a robust set of features to ensure the security of your information and adherence to relevant regulations. Here's a closer look:

Security Features:

- **User Authentication and Authorization:** SharePoint leverages Azure Active Directory for user authentication and authorization. This ensures only authorized users can access SharePoint and controls the level of access (read, edit, delete) each user has for specific sites, libraries, or lists.

- **Permission Levels:** Granular permission levels allow you to define exactly what actions users can perform on content. You can set permissions at different levels, like site collection, site, library/list, or even individual items.

- **Data Loss Prevention (DLP):** SharePoint DLP helps prevent sensitive information leaks. DLP policies can be configured to identify and restrict users from sharing confidential data via email, downloads, or unauthorized channels.

- **Encryption at Rest and in Transit:** Data stored in SharePoint is encrypted at rest and in transit. This means data is scrambled both when it's stored on Microsoft servers and while it's being transferred between your device and SharePoint.

- **Auditing and Logging:** SharePoint maintains comprehensive audit logs that track user activity, including what actions were performed, on what items, and by whom. This audit trail is crucial for security investigations and compliance purposes.

Compliance Considerations:

- **Industry Regulations:** Depending on your industry, you might need to comply with specific data privacy regulations like GDPR (General Data Protection Regulation) or HIPAA (Health Insurance Portability and Accountability Act). SharePoint offers features to help manage data in accordance with these regulations.

- **Data Residency:** For some organizations, data residency regulations mandate that data be stored within specific geographic locations. SharePoint offers options to choose the data residency region that aligns with your compliance requirements.

- **eDiscovery:** SharePoint's eDiscovery capabilities allow you to identify, search, and export relevant electronic data in response to legal or regulatory requests.

Benefits of SharePoint Security and Compliance:

- **Data Protection:** The security features in SharePoint safeguard your sensitive information from unauthorized access, leaks, or breaches.

- **Compliance Assurance:** SharePoint helps organizations meet various industry regulations and data privacy requirements.

- **Enhanced Security Posture:** Regular security updates and monitoring by Microsoft contribute to a more robust security posture for your SharePoint environment.

- **Audit Trails for Accountability:** Audit logs provide transparency and accountability for user actions within SharePoint.

Remember: Security is an ongoing process. It's crucial to stay informed about potential threats, implement security best practices, and conduct regular security audits to maintain a strong security posture for your SharePoint environment.

CHAPTER FIVE
CUSTOMIZING SHAREPOINT

Branding and Themes

SharePoint offers functionalities to customize the look and feel of your sites, allowing you to create a visually appealing and brand-consistent user experience. Here's how branding and themes come into play:

Branding:

- **Represents the identity of your organization.** This encompasses your logo, colour palette, fonts, and overall visual style.

Themes in SharePoint:

- **Act as a way to apply your brand elements to your SharePoint sites.** Themes define the visual aspects you see on a SharePoint site, including:

    - **Colours:** Align with your brand's colour scheme to create a recognizable identity.

    - **Fonts:** Use fonts consistent with your branding for a unified look and feel.

    - **Logos:** Display your organization's logo prominently within the site.

- o **Backgrounds:** Set background colours or images that complement your brand identity.

- o **Navigation:** Customize the navigation structure and style to match your brand and website.

Benefits of Branding Your SharePoint Sites:

- **Improved User Experience:** A well-branded SharePoint site creates a professional and familiar experience for users, fostering trust and engagement.

- **Enhanced Brand Recognition:** Consistent branding across all your digital platforms, including SharePoint, reinforces your brand identity and strengthens recognition.

- **Increased User Adoption:** A visually appealing and user-friendly SharePoint site encourages users to adopt the platform for collaboration and communication.

- **Boosted Employee Morale:** A branded SharePoint environment that reflects the company culture can contribute to a stronger sense of belonging and employee morale.

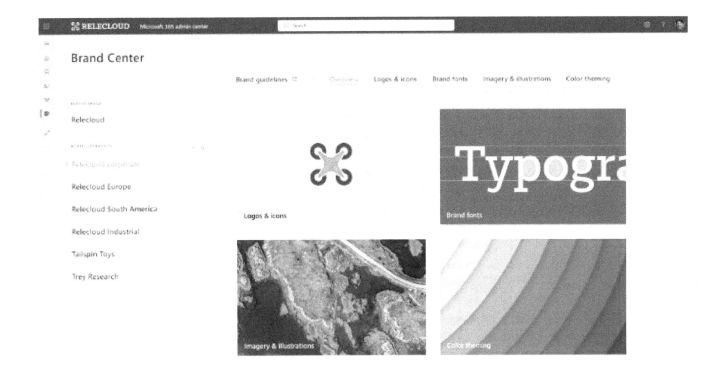

How to Brand Your SharePoint Site:

- **Identify your brand guidelines:** Start by clearly defining your organization's brand colours, fonts, logo, and any other visual style elements.

- **Choose a theming approach:** SharePoint offers a few options for creating themes:

    - **Use pre-built themes:** Microsoft provides a library of pre-designed themes you can use as a starting point.

    - **Customize existing themes:** Modify the colours, fonts, and layouts of pre-built themes to better match your brand.

    - **Create a custom theme:** For complete control over the look and feel, you can develop a custom theme using CSS (Cascading Style Sheets).

Best Practices for Branding SharePoint:

- **Maintain consistency:** Ensure your branding elements are applied uniformly across all your SharePoint sites and subsites.

- **Balance visual appeal with usability:** While branding is important, prioritize a clear and functional site layout to avoid hindering user experience.

- **Accessibility considerations:** Make sure your colour choices and font styles meet accessibility guidelines to ensure inclusivity for all users.

By effectively utilizing branding and themes in SharePoint, you can create a visually appealing and user-friendly platform that strengthens your brand identity, improves user experience, and ultimately drives better adoption and collaboration within your organization.

Site Customization

Beyond branding and themes, SharePoint offers a rich set of customization options to tailor your sites to your specific needs and workflows. Here's a deeper dive into what you can achieve:

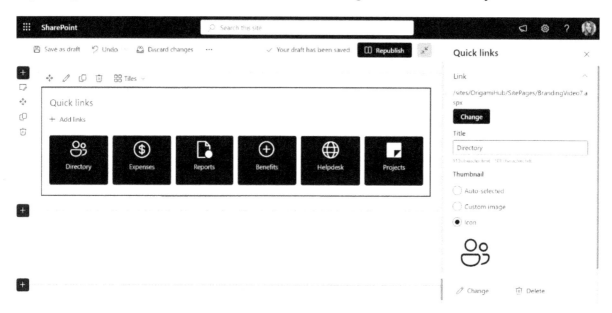

Customizing Navigation:

- **Out-of-the-box navigation:** SharePoint provides default navigation options like top navigation bars and quick launch menus. You can arrange and configure these to suit your site structure.

- **Custom navigation links:** Add custom links to relevant internal or external web pages to provide users with easy access to essential resources.

- **Mega menus:** Create comprehensive drop-down menus to organize a large number of navigation links effectively, preventing clutter in the main interface.

Customizing Lists and Libraries:

- **Views:** Create different views of the same list or library data. Filter and sort information based on specific criteria to cater to different user needs.

- **Calculated columns:** Generate new data points within list items using formulas based on existing information in the list. This can automate calculations and provide valuable insights.

- **Conditional formatting:** Apply formatting rules to rows or columns within lists. This can involve highlighting specific data points based on conditions, making it easier to identify trends or exceptions at a glance.

Adding Custom Pages and Web Parts:

- **Page layouts:** SharePoint offers pre-designed page layouts with different sections and column arrangements. You can choose a layout that best suits the content you want to present.

- **Custom web parts:** In addition to the pre-built web parts, you can leverage SharePoint Framework to develop custom web parts that cater to your unique requirements. These web parts can display specific data, functionalities, or integrations not readily available with out-of-the-box options.

Leveraging Content Types:

- **Define reusable templates:** Create content types to establish a standardized structure for specific content categories. This ensures consistency and simplifies content creation for users.

- **Content type features:** Associate specific features like workflows or custom columns with different content types. This automates repetitive tasks and streamlines content management processes for different content categories.

Benefits of Site Customization:

- **Improved User Experience:** Tailored navigation, views, and layouts make it easier for users to find the information they need and navigate the site efficiently.

- **Enhanced Functionality:** Customizations like calculated columns and workflows automate tasks and improve the overall functionality of your SharePoint site.

- **Streamlined Workflows:** By configuring views and leveraging custom web parts, you can design workflows that align perfectly with your team's processes.

- **Increased User Adoption:** A user-friendly and well-organized SharePoint site encourages users to take advantage of the platform for collaboration and communication.

Important Considerations for Customization:

- **Usability first:** While customization offers flexibility, prioritize a clear and intuitive site structure to avoid overwhelming users.

- **Information architecture:** Plan your information architecture beforehand to ensure a logical organization of content and easy navigation for users.

- **Governance and consistency:** If allowing some level of customization for sub-sites, establish guidelines to maintain overall consistency and user experience across your SharePoint environment.

By strategically using SharePoint's customization capabilities, you can create an intuitive and feature-rich platform that caters to your organization's specific needs, ultimately boosting user adoption, streamlining workflows, and fostering better collaboration within your teams.

Custom Web Parts

SharePoint out-of-the-box offers a variety of web parts that you can add to pages to display information, data, and functionalities. But what if those pre-built options don't perfectly match your specific needs? That's where custom web parts come in!

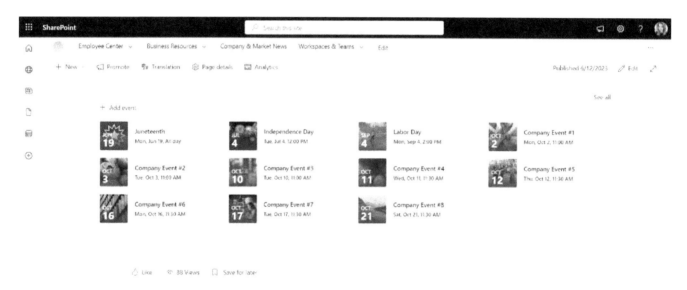

Custom web parts are essentially reusable UI components that you can develop to extend the functionalities of SharePoint beyond its default capabilities. They allow you to display data, perform actions, and interact with users in ways that aren't available with standard web parts.

Here's a breakdown of what custom web parts are and how they can benefit you:

- **Built using SharePoint Framework (SPFx):** SPFx is a Microsoft development framework specifically designed for creating custom extensions and add-ins for SharePoint. It provides the tools and libraries you need to build robust and user-friendly web parts.

- **Tailored Functionalities:** The beauty of custom web parts lies in their ability to address your unique requirements. You can create web parts to:

- Display data from external systems that aren't natively supported by SharePoint.

- Automate tasks and workflows specific to your team's processes.

- Integrate with third-party applications to enhance collaboration capabilities.

- Provide interactive features or visualizations not available with standard web parts.

- **Improved User Experience:** Well-designed custom web parts can streamline user workflows and make it easier for users to find the information or perform actions they need within SharePoint.

- **Examples of Custom Web Parts:**

  - A custom web part that displays real-time sales data from your CRM system directly within SharePoint.

  - A web part that automates a document approval process, routing documents for review and collecting feedback.

  - A custom calendar web part that integrates with your scheduling software, providing a unified view of your team's appointments.

Development Considerations:

- **Technical Expertise:** Building custom web parts requires programming knowledge and familiarity with SharePoint Framework. If you don't have in-house development resources, you can consider hiring external developers or leverage pre-built web part solutions from third-party vendors.

- **Maintenance and Updates:** Custom web parts need to be maintained and updated to ensure compatibility with future SharePoint versions and security patches.

Overall, custom web parts offer a powerful way to extend the capabilities of SharePoint and tailor it to your organization's specific needs. By carefully considering the development requirements and ongoing maintenance, custom web parts can be a valuable asset for enhancing user experience, streamlining workflows, and boosting overall SharePoint adoption within your teams.

Power Apps and Power Automate Integration

In the world of Microsoft Power Platform, Power Apps and Power Automate work together seamlessly to create a dynamic and automated user experience within SharePoint. Here's how this powerful integration works:

Power Apps:

- Imagine them as: Customizable canvas apps that allow you to build user interfaces for data collection, task management, or process automation. Think of them as the building blocks for creating user-friendly interfaces within SharePoint.

Power Automate:

- Think of them as: The automation engine behind the scenes. Power Automate creates workflows that can trigger actions based on events or user interactions. These workflows can connect to various data sources, including SharePoint lists and libraries.

Integration Benefits:

- **Enhanced User Experience:** Power Apps provide a user-friendly interface for interacting with SharePoint data. You can create custom forms, dashboards, or data visualizations that are more intuitive than traditional SharePoint interfaces.

- **Streamlined Workflows:** Power Automate automates tasks triggered by user interactions within your Power Apps. This eliminates manual data entry, reduces errors, and streamlines overall processes.

- **Flexibility:** The combined power of Power Apps and Power Automate allows you to build highly customized solutions that perfectly match your specific business needs. You can connect to various data sources, automate complex workflows, and create a user experience tailored to your team.

How it Works:

1. **User Interaction in Power Apps:** A user interacts with your Power App, perhaps submitting data through a form or triggering an action.

2. **Power Automate Workflow Trigger:** This user interaction triggers a workflow defined within Power Automate.

3. **Workflow Actions:** The workflow performs a series of pre-defined actions. These actions can involve:

   - Updating data within SharePoint lists or libraries.

   - Sending notifications or emails.

43

- o Integrating with other applications or services.

- o Triggering further actions within Power Automate for complex processes.

Examples of Integration:

- **Expense Reporting App:** Build a Power App for employees to submit expense reports. Upon submission, Power Automate triggers a workflow that routes the report for approval and automatically updates a SharePoint list with the expense details.

- **Leave Request Approval:** Create a Power App for submitting leave requests. Power Automate can initiate a workflow to route the request to managers for approval, update a leave calendar in SharePoint, and send notifications to all parties involved.

- **Customer Onboarding App:** Develop a Power App to capture new customer information. Power Automate can automate tasks like creating customer records in SharePoint, sending welcome emails, and triggering further actions in your CRM system.

Overall, the integration between Power Apps and Power Automate unlocks a new level of functionality within SharePoint. By combining the user-friendly interfaces of Power Apps with the automation capabilities of Power Automate, you can create powerful solutions that streamline workflows, improve user experience, and empower your teams to be more productive within your SharePoint environment.

CHAPTER SIX
MICROSOFT SHAREPOINT

User Management

SharePoint user management involves creating, configuring, and assigning permissions to users who access your SharePoint sites and content. Here's a breakdown of the key concepts:

Users and Groups:

- **Users:** Individual people who need access to SharePoint. They can be internal users within your organization or external guests.

- **Groups:** Collections of users who are assigned permissions collectively. This simplifies permission management, as you can assign permissions to a group rather than individual users for specific sites or content.

User Accounts:

- **Synchronization:** SharePoint user accounts are typically synchronized with your organization's Azure Active Directory (Azure AD). This ensures users only need one set of credentials to access various Microsoft applications, including SharePoint.

- **User Profiles:** SharePoint user profiles store additional information about users beyond their login credentials. This can include contact details, department affiliation, and even a profile picture.

Permissions and Access Levels:

- **Permissions define what a user can do within a SharePoint site or with specific content.** SharePoint offers different permission levels with varying degrees of access, such as:

  - **Read:** Allows users to view content but not edit or modify it.

  - **Edit:** Grants permission to edit and update content.

  - **Contribute:** Allows users to create new content and edit existing items but not manage permissions.

  - **Full Control:** Provides complete control over a site or content, including permission management.

Assigning Permissions:

- **Permissions can be assigned to individual users or groups.** This allows you to grant granular access control based on user roles and responsibilities within your organization.

- **Inheritance:** Permissions can be inherited from a parent site to its sub-sites. This simplifies management but can be overridden if necessary to grant specific permissions at a sub-site level.

Security Considerations:

- **Principle of Least Privilege:** It's crucial to follow the principle of least privilege. Grant users only the minimum permissions they need to perform their tasks effectively. This minimizes security risks and accidental data modification.

- **Reviewing Permissions Regularly:** User roles and responsibilities can change over time. Regularly review and update permissions to ensure continued security and access control.

Benefits of Effective User Management:

- **Enhanced Security:** Granular permission control ensures only authorized users have access to sensitive information.

- **Improved Collaboration:** Streamlined access based on user roles fosters better collaboration within teams.

- **Reduced Administration Overhead:** Managing permissions through groups simplifies administration compared to assigning permissions to every user individually.

- **Increased User Productivity:** Clear access to relevant information and functionalities empowers users to be more productive.

By implementing a well-defined user management strategy, you can ensure secure access to SharePoint for your users, optimize collaboration, and maintain control over your organization's data within the platform.

Site and Storage Management

Effective site and storage management are fundamental aspects of keeping your SharePoint environment organized, efficient, and secure. Here's a closer look at the key considerations for both:

Site Management:

- **Site Lifecycle Management:**

  - **Planning:** Define a clear purpose and target audience for each SharePoint site before creation.

  - **Creation:** Utilize templates and best practices to establish a well-structured information architecture from the start.

- o **Use:** Monitor site activity and content usage to identify opportunities for improvement or consolidation.

- o **Disposition:** Have a plan for archiving inactive sites or deleting obsolete ones to maintain a clean and organized SharePoint environment.

- **Content Organization:**

  - o **Folders and Libraries:** Organize content logically using folders within libraries for specific categories or project types.

  - o **Metadata and Tags:** Implement a consistent metadata tagging system to categorize content effectively and facilitate searchability.

  - o **Content Types:** Create reusable content types for specific information categories to ensure consistency and streamline content creation.

- **Site Governance:**

  - o **Usage Policies:** Establish clear guidelines for how users should create, manage, and share content within SharePoint.

  - o **Versioning and Retention:** Define versioning policies to track changes and determine how long different content types need to be retained.

  - o **Site Permissions:** Implement a role-based permission structure to grant users access based on their needs and responsibilities.

Storage Management:

- **Understanding Storage Limits:** SharePoint plans come with a certain amount of storage allocated per user or organization.

- **Monitoring Storage Usage:** Track your storage consumption to identify trends and potential bottlenecks.

- **Optimizing Storage:**

  - o **File Compression:** Compress large files before uploading them to SharePoint to reduce storage space.

  - o **Inactive Content Archiving:** Move inactive or less frequently accessed content to external archives to free up space on SharePoint.

  - o **Content Deletion:** Regularly review and delete obsolete or redundant content to optimize storage usage.

Benefits of Effective Site and Storage Management:

- **Improved User Experience:** A well-organized SharePoint environment with clear structures and findable information makes it easier for users to collaborate and access what they need.

- **Enhanced Collaboration:** Clear governance policies and consistent content organization promote better teamwork and knowledge sharing.

- **Reduced Costs:** Optimizing storage through compression, archiving, and deletion helps you stay within your storage limits and avoid exceeding quotas.

- **Increased Security:** Proper user permissions and lifecycle management practices minimize security risks and unauthorized access to sensitive information.

By following these site and storage management best practices, you can create a user-friendly, efficient, and secure SharePoint environment that empowers your teams to collaborate effectively and maximize the value of your organization's data.

Monitoring and Reporting

In SharePoint, monitoring and reporting go hand-in-hand, providing valuable insights into user activity, site health, and overall platform usage. Here's how these functionalities work together:

Monitoring:

- **Tracks various aspects of your SharePoint environment:** This includes user activity, site performance, search queries, and potential errors.

- **Proactive identification of issues:** By continuously monitoring key metrics, you can proactively identify potential problems before they disrupt user experience or cause data loss.

- **Tools for Monitoring:** SharePoint offers built-in monitoring tools like SharePoint Health Analyzer and auditing logs. You can also leverage third-party monitoring solutions for more comprehensive insights.

Reporting:

- **Transforms monitoring data into actionable information:** Monitoring data is valuable, but reports help you analyse trends, identify patterns, and make informed decisions about your SharePoint environment.

- **Usage Reports:** Track how users interact with SharePoint, including which sites and content are most popular, what types of devices users access from, and common search queries.

- **Performance Reports:** Monitor server health, identify performance bottlenecks, and ensure optimal uptime and responsiveness for your users.

- **Compliance Reports:** Generate reports to ensure adherence to relevant regulations and data privacy requirements.

Benefits of Monitoring and Reporting:

- **Improved User Experience:** By identifying and resolving issues proactively, you can ensure a smooth and efficient user experience within SharePoint.

- **Data-Driven Decisions:** Reports provide valuable insights to optimize your SharePoint environment, allocate resources effectively, and make data-driven decisions for future improvements.

- **Enhanced Security:** Monitoring user activity and identifying potential security threats helps you maintain a secure SharePoint environment.

- **Improved Collaboration:** Understanding how users interact with content can inform strategies to improve collaboration and knowledge sharing within your teams.

Here are some additional points to consider for effective monitoring and reporting:

- **Define Key Performance Indicators (KPIs):** Determine the metrics that matter most for your specific SharePoint usage and user needs.

- **Schedule Regular Reports:** Set up automated reports to be generated at regular intervals for consistent monitoring and analysis.

- **Take Actionable Steps:** Don't just generate reports; translate insights into concrete actions to improve your SharePoint environment.

By implementing a robust monitoring and reporting strategy, you can gain valuable visibility into your SharePoint platform, identify areas for improvement, and ultimately optimize your environment to empower your users and maximize the return on your SharePoint investment.

Backup and Recovery

In the realm of SharePoint, having a well-defined backup and recovery strategy is crucial to safeguard your data from accidental deletion, hardware malfunctions, security breaches, or even ransomware attacks. Here's a breakdown of the essential elements for robust backup and recovery:

Backup Options:

- **Native SharePoint Backup:** SharePoint offers built-in backup functionalities for site collections and specific components. This is a suitable option for basic backups, but it may lack automation and flexibility for comprehensive data protection.

- **Third-Party Backup Solutions:** Numerous third-party vendors offer robust backup solutions specifically designed for SharePoint. These solutions often provide features like automated backups, granular recovery options, and long-term data retention.

Backup Strategies:

- **Full Backups vs. Incremental Backups:** Regularly perform full backups to capture your entire SharePoint environment at a specific point in time. Supplement these with frequent incremental backups to capture only changes made since the last full backup.

- **Backup Scheduling:** Establish a consistent backup schedule that balances the need for frequent backups with storage considerations. Daily backups are often recommended, but you might adjust the frequency based on your specific data volume and risk tolerance.

- **Backup Verification:** Don't assume your backups are functional until you test them! Regularly perform test restores to ensure your backups can be retrieved and used successfully in case of a disaster.

Recovery Process:

- **Recovery Options:** The specific recovery method depends on the nature of data loss. SharePoint offers options to restore entire site collections, individual items, or specific versions of files. Third-party backup solutions might provide more granular recovery options.

- **Disaster Recovery Plan:** Having a documented disaster recovery plan in place is crucial for minimizing downtime and ensuring a swift recovery process in case of a major outage. Your plan should outline roles, responsibilities, and the steps to be taken for restoring your SharePoint environment.

Additional Considerations:

- **Security of Backups:** Store your backups securely, ideally in a separate location from your primary SharePoint environment. This protects your backups from being affected by the same incident that caused data loss on your main system.

- **Version Control:** SharePoint's built-in versioning history allows you to recover previous versions of files. This can be helpful in case of accidental edits or overwritten content.

- **Compliance Requirements:** Depending on your industry regulations, you might have specific data retention requirements. Factor these requirements into your backup strategy to ensure compliance.

Benefits of a Strong Backup and Recovery Strategy:

- **Peace of Mind:** Knowing your data is protected gives you peace of mind and minimizes the risk of permanent data loss.

- **Disaster Preparedness:** A robust backup and recovery plan ensures you can restore your SharePoint environment quickly and efficiently in case of unforeseen circumstances.

- **Business Continuity:** Minimized downtime due to data loss safeguards business continuity and keeps your operations running smoothly.

- **Data Security:** Backups provide an additional layer of security by offering a means to recover data even in the event of a security breach or ransomware attack.

By implementing a comprehensive backup and recovery strategy that leverages both native SharePoint functionalities and third-party solutions if needed, you can ensure the availability and integrity of your data within your SharePoint environment. This proactive approach safeguards your information and fosters business continuity in the face of potential data loss scenarios.

CHAPTER SEVEN
SHAREPOINT FOR DEVELOPERS

SharePoint Framework (SPFx)

SharePoint Framework (SPFx) is a Microsoft development model that allows you to extend the functionalities of SharePoint and Microsoft Teams using modern web technologies. It essentially empowers you to create custom web parts, extensions, and applications that seamlessly integrate with these platforms.

Here's a closer look at what SPFx offers:

- **Modern Web Technologies:** SPFx leverages JavaScript, HTML, and CSS, providing a familiar development environment for web developers. This simplifies the creation of custom components that align perfectly with the look and feel of modern SharePoint experiences.

- **Rich Set of Features:** SPFx enables you to develop a variety of components, including:

  - **Custom web parts:** Extend SharePoint's built-in functionalities by creating web parts that display specific data, perform actions, or interact with users in unique ways.

  - **Extensions:** Enhance SharePoint with custom extensions that modify the user interface, add functionalities to existing lists or libraries, or integrate with external data sources.

  - **Microsoft Teams Apps:** Develop custom applications that extend the capabilities of Microsoft Teams, fostering improved collaboration and communication within your teams.

- **Benefits of Using SPFx:**

  - **Improved User Experience:** Create custom solutions that address your specific needs and streamline workflows for your users within SharePoint and Teams.

  - **Increased Productivity:** Well-designed custom components can automate tasks, improve data visualization, and empower users to be more productive.

  - **Enhanced Collaboration:** Foster better teamwork and knowledge sharing by creating custom tools that cater to your team's communication and collaboration needs.

  - **Seamless Integration:** SPFx components integrate smoothly with the overall SharePoint and Teams experience, maintaining a unified user interface.

- **Development Considerations:**

  - **Learning Curve:** While SPFx leverages familiar web technologies, there's still a learning curve involved in understanding the SharePoint object model and development framework.

  - **Development Resources:** Building custom SPFx components requires programming expertise. If you don't have in-house development resources, consider partnering with external developers or leveraging pre-built solutions from third-party vendors.

In essence, SharePoint Framework empowers developers to unlock the full potential of SharePoint and Microsoft Teams. By creating custom components that cater to your organization's specific needs, you can streamline workflows, improve user experience, and foster a more collaborative and productive work environment.

APIs and Web Services

SharePoint offers robust capabilities for interacting with data and functionalities through APIs (Application Programming Interfaces) and web services. These functionalities allow you to integrate SharePoint with other applications, extend its features, and automate workflows. Here's a breakdown of what APIs and web services provide in SharePoint:

APIs (Application Programming Interfaces):

- **Act as intermediaries:** APIs provide a programmatic way for external applications to interact with SharePoint data and functionalities.

- **REST API:** SharePoint's primary API is the REST API, which utilizes a standardized approach based on web technologies like HTTP verbs (GET, POST, PUT, DELETE) and JSON or XML for data formatting.

- **Benefits of using REST API:**

  - **Flexibility:** The REST API allows you to integrate SharePoint with a wide range of applications and services that support web APIs.

  - **Standardized Approach:** The REST interface simplifies development as it follows widely adopted web standards.

  - **Automation Potential:** By leveraging the REST API, you can automate tasks and workflows by programmatically interacting with SharePoint data.

Web Services:

- **Another method for interaction:** While APIs offer a more modern approach, SharePoint also offers web services for communication and data exchange. These web services typically use SOAP (Simple Object Access Protocol) for communication and XML for data formatting.

- **Maturity of Web Services:** Web services have been around longer than REST APIs and might be used in some older custom integrations with SharePoint.

- **Gradual Shift:** Microsoft is moving towards the REST API as the primary method for interaction, and new development should prioritize using the REST API over web services.

Use Cases for APIs and Web Services:

- **Custom Application Integration:** Integrate SharePoint with other business applications like CRM systems, ERP systems, or custom-developed tools to create a more unified data environment.

- **Data Migration and Synchronization:** Leverage APIs to automate data migration between SharePoint and other platforms or to synchronize data for real-time consistency.

- **Workflow Automation:** Develop custom workflows using APIs to automate tasks triggered by specific events or user interactions within SharePoint.

- **External Content Display:** Utilize APIs to display data from external sources directly within SharePoint dashboards or custom web parts.

Benefits of Utilizing APIs and Web Services:

- **Enhanced Functionality:** Extend SharePoint's capabilities beyond its out-of-the-box features by integrating with other applications and services.

- **Improved Efficiency:** Automate manual tasks and workflows through programmatic interaction with SharePoint data.

- **Streamlined Processes:** Integrate SharePoint with your existing business systems to create a more efficient and connected work environment.

- **Development Flexibility:** APIs and web services provide a powerful foundation for developers to build custom solutions that cater to your organization's specific needs.

Security Considerations:

- **API Permissions:** When using APIs, implement proper access controls and permissions to ensure only authorized applications can interact with your SharePoint data.

- **Data Security:** Be mindful of the data you expose through APIs and take measures to protect sensitive information.

By understanding and leveraging the capabilities of APIs and web services, you can unlock the full potential of SharePoint as a platform for collaboration, data management, and process automation within your organization.

Developing Custom Solutions

Here's a comprehensive overview of developing custom solutions in SharePoint:

Approaches to Custom Development:

- **Out-of-the-Box Options:** SharePoint offers a variety of built-in features and functionalities that you can leverage to create solutions without extensive coding. This includes:

  o **Site branding and themes:** Create a visually appealing and consistent user experience for your SharePoint sites.

  o **Custom navigation:** Organize and structure your site navigation to match your specific needs.

  o **Custom views and lists:** Tailor how information is displayed and organized within lists and libraries.

  o **Power Apps and Power Automate:** Build user-friendly interfaces and automate workflows using these no-code/low-code tools.

- **SharePoint Framework (SPFx):** For more advanced customization beyond built-in features, SPFx provides a powerful development framework. SPFx allows you to create custom web parts, extensions, and applications that seamlessly integrate with SharePoint and Microsoft Teams. Here's what SPFx development involves:

  o **Programming Languages:** SPFx utilizes JavaScript, HTML, and CSS, offering a familiar environment for web developers.

  o **Development Tools:** Microsoft provides tools and libraries specifically designed for SPFx development, simplifying the creation of custom components.

  o **Learning Curve:** While leveraging familiar technologies, understanding the SharePoint object model and development framework requires some investment in learning.

   ○ **Development Resources:** If you don't have in-house development expertise, consider partnering with external developers or using pre-built SPFx solutions from third-party vendors.

Alternatives to Custom Development:

- **Third-Party Add-Ins:** Explore the vast marketplace of pre-built SharePoint add-ins that address various functionalities. These add-ins can often fulfil your needs without extensive custom development.

- **Consulting Services:** Partner with experienced SharePoint consulting firms that can assess your requirements, recommend solutions, and potentially develop custom solutions if necessary.

Choosing the Right Approach:

The best approach for developing custom SharePoint solutions depends on several factors:

- **Complexity of Requirements:** Simpler needs might be met with out-of-the-box features or third-party add-ins, while complex functionalities might necessitate custom development using SPFx.

- **Development Resources:** In-house development expertise plays a crucial role. If you lack the resources, consider pre-built solutions or consulting partners.

- **Long-Term Maintenance:** Custom solutions require ongoing maintenance to ensure compatibility with future SharePoint updates and security patches. Factor in the maintenance commitment when making your decision.

Benefits of Custom Development:

- **Tailored Functionality:** Custom solutions perfectly match your organization's specific needs and workflows, leading to improved efficiency and user experience.

- **Enhanced Integration:** Develop custom integrations with other applications and data sources to create a unified work environment.

- **Competitive Advantage:** Custom solutions can give your organization a competitive edge by streamlining processes and empowering users with unique functionalities.

Developing custom solutions in SharePoint empowers you to create a platform that perfectly aligns with your organization's needs. By carefully evaluating your requirements, choosing the right development approach, and considering the long-term implications, you can leverage custom development to unlock the full potential of SharePoint and achieve your collaboration and productivity goals.

Integrating Third-Party Applications

Integrating third-party applications with SharePoint broadens its functionalities and connects it to the wider business ecosystem you rely on. Here's how you can achieve this:

Understanding Integration Methods:

- **Out-of-the-Box Connectors:** SharePoint offers built-in connectors for various popular applications like Microsoft Teams, Power BI, and Dropbox. These connectors enable basic data sharing and synchronization between SharePoint and those applications.

- **Custom API Integration:** For deeper integration beyond pre-built connectors, leverage APIs (Application Programming Interfaces) provided by third-party applications. SharePoint's REST API allows you to programmatically interact with data and functionalities of these applications.

- **Third-Party Add-Ins:** The SharePoint Store offers a rich marketplace of third-party add-ins that integrate various applications with SharePoint. These add-ins provide pre-built functionality and often require minimal configuration to set up.

Popular Integration Scenarios:

- **Line-of-Business Systems:** Integrate SharePoint with CRM systems, ERP systems, or other business-critical applications to create a unified platform for data management and collaboration.

- **Content Management Systems (CMS):** Connect SharePoint with your CMS to streamline document management workflows and ensure consistent content across platforms.

- **External Data Sources:** Tap into data from external databases or web services using APIs to display relevant information within SharePoint dashboards or reports.

- **Productivity Tools:** Enhance collaboration by integrating project management tools, communication platforms, or e-signature services with SharePoint.

Benefits of Third-Party Application Integration:

- **Extended Functionality:** Empower users with a wider range of tools and functionalities within the familiar SharePoint environment.

- **Improved Efficiency:** Streamline workflows by connecting SharePoint with the applications your teams already use.

- **Centralized Data Management:** Consolidate information from various sources into a central location for better accessibility and data governance.

- **Enhanced Collaboration:** Foster better teamwork by enabling seamless collaboration across different applications.

Security Considerations:

- **API Permissions:** When using APIs, implement proper access controls to ensure only authorized applications can interact with your SharePoint data.

- **Data Security:** Be mindful of the data you expose through integrations and take measures to protect sensitive information.

- **Third-Party Vendor Trust:** Choose reputable third-party vendors with a proven track record of security and data privacy practices.

Choosing the Right Integration Approach:

The best method for integrating third-party applications depends on your specific needs and technical expertise:

- **Out-of-the-Box Connectors:** Simple integration needs for popular applications can often be met with built-in connectors.

- **Custom API Integration:** For complex integrations or unique requirements, custom development using APIs might be necessary, but it requires programming expertise.

- **Third-Party Add-Ins:** A vast array of pre-built add-ins offer a user-friendly and efficient way to integrate various applications with SharePoint, often with minimal setup.

By carefully considering your needs, security, and technical resources, you can leverage third-party application integration to empower your users, streamline workflows, and maximize the value of SharePoint within your organization's ecosystem.

CHAPTER EIGHT
ADVANCED SHAREPOINT TOPICS

Enterprise Content Management (ECM)

Enterprise Content Management (ECM) refers to a set of strategies and technologies that organizations use to capture, store, manage, secure, and ultimately leverage all forms of information throughout its lifecycle. In simpler terms, it's an all-encompassing approach to managing your organization's digital content, from the moment it's created to its eventual disposition.

Here are some key aspects of ECM:

- **Content Types:** ECM systems can handle various content types, including documents, emails, images, videos, social media posts, and more.

- **Document Management:** ECM provides features for document version control, access control, and automated workflows to streamline document lifecycles.

- **Content Storage and Retrieval:** ECM systems offer secure storage for your organization's content and efficient retrieval mechanisms to find information quickly and easily.

- **Collaboration:** ECM fosters collaboration by allowing teams to work on documents simultaneously, share content securely, and track changes.

- **Security and Compliance:** ECM systems provide robust security features to protect sensitive information and ensure adherence to industry regulations and data privacy laws.

Benefits of Implementing ECM:

- **Improved Productivity:** By streamlining document management and content retrieval, ECM empowers users to find information faster and work more efficiently.

- **Enhanced Collaboration:** ECM fosters better teamwork by providing a central platform for document sharing and collaboration.

- **Reduced Costs:** ECM can help reduce storage costs by eliminating redundant or obsolete content, and improve operational efficiency.

- **Increased Compliance:** ECM systems help organizations meet regulatory requirements and ensure data security.

- **Improved Decision Making:** ECM facilitates better access to information, which can lead to more informed decision-making across the organization.

Here are some common examples of how ECM is used in organizations:

- **Human Resources:** Managing employee onboarding documents, performance reviews, and training materials.

- **Finance:** Storing and managing financial documents, invoices, and contracts.

- **Sales and Marketing:** Creating and sharing sales proposals, marketing collateral, and customer information.

- **Legal:** Managing legal documents, contracts, and intellectual property.

ECM vs SharePoint:

While SharePoint offers some ECM capabilities, it's not a full-fledged ECM system. SharePoint excels at collaboration and document management within Microsoft 365, but it might lack some advanced features like robust legal holds or comprehensive content archiving functionalities that some ECM systems offer.

Choosing the Right ECM Solution:

The ideal ECM solution depends on your organization's specific needs, budget, and technical expertise. Here are some factors to consider:

- **Content Types:** Evaluate the types of content you need to manage and ensure the ECM system can handle them effectively.

- **Scalability:** Consider your organization's growth and choose a solution that can scale to meet your future needs.

- **Security:** Select an ECM system with robust security features to protect your sensitive information.

- **Integration:** Ensure the ECM system integrates seamlessly with your existing applications and workflows.

- **Ease of Use:** Choose a user-friendly system that your employees can adopt easily.

By implementing a well-defined ECM strategy and selecting the right solution, you can gain control over your organization's content, improve collaboration, and unlock the full potential of your information assets.

Business Intelligence and Dashboards

In the realm of business intelligence (BI), dashboards are visual representations of key performance indicators (KPIs) and other data insights that provide users with a quick and comprehensive understanding of an organization's performance. Here's a breakdown of how BI dashboards function within SharePoint:

Business Intelligence (BI):

- **Transforming Data into Insights:** BI is a broad discipline that involves collecting, analysing, and interpreting data to reveal trends, patterns, and actionable insights for better business decision-making.

- **Data Warehouses and Cubes:** BI tools often leverage data warehouses or cubes to store and organize vast amounts of data from various sources in a way that facilitates analysis.

- **Benefits of BI:** Effective BI empowers organizations to:

    o Identify areas for improvement and make data-driven decisions.

    o Track progress towards goals and objectives.

    o Improve operational efficiency and resource allocation.

    o Gain a competitive edge through data-driven insights.

SharePoint and BI Dashboards:

- **Leveraging Existing Data:** SharePoint often serves as a central repository for various types of organizational data. BI tools can connect to SharePoint data sources to extract relevant information for analysis and dashboard creation.

- **Third-Party BI Tools:** Several third-party BI tools integrate seamlessly with SharePoint, allowing you to create compelling dashboards directly within the SharePoint environment. Microsoft Power BI is a popular option that offers a robust set of features for data visualization and dashboard creation.

- **Benefits of BI Dashboards in SharePoint:**

    o **Improved User Experience:** Visual dashboards present complex data in an easy-to-understand format, making information readily accessible to users.

    o **Enhanced Collaboration:** Shared dashboards foster data-driven discussions and collaborative decision-making.

    o **Actionable Insights:** Dashboards empower users to identify trends, track progress, and take timely actions based on the insights presented.

Key Elements of Effective BI Dashboards:

- **Clear Focus:** Each dashboard should have a well-defined purpose and target audience.

- **Relevant KPIs:** Select KPIs that accurately represent the success metrics for a specific area or process.

- **Visualizations:** Utilize charts, graphs, and other visual elements to present data in an engaging and informative way.

- **Interactivity:** Consider interactive features that allow users to drill down into specific data points for further analysis.

- **Regular Updates:** Ensure dashboards are updated regularly to reflect the latest data and maintain user trust.

Overall, BI dashboards within SharePoint empower you to transform your data into actionable insights, facilitate data-driven decision making, and ultimately improve business performance across your organization.

Data Governance and Compliance

Data governance and compliance are fundamental aspects of managing information within SharePoint. Here's a closer look at how these two concepts work together:

Data Governance

- **Overall Data Management Strategy:** Data governance establishes a framework for how your organization manages its data throughout its lifecycle, from creation to storage, access, and eventual disposition.

- **Key Components:** Effective data governance in SharePoint involves:

  - **Data Classification:** Classifying data based on its sensitivity (confidential, public, etc.) to determine appropriate security measures and access controls.

  - **Policies and Procedures:** Creating clear policies and procedures regarding data ownership, usage, retention, and disposal to ensure consistent data management practices.

  - **User Roles and Permissions:** Implementing a role-based access control system to grant users access to data based on their job functions and responsibilities.

  - **Data Monitoring and Auditing:** Monitoring user activity, tracking data access, and auditing changes to ensure data security and identify potential issues.

Data Compliance

- **Adherence to Regulations:** Data compliance focuses on adhering to relevant laws and regulations that govern data privacy, security, and record-keeping within your industry or region. Examples include GDPR (General Data Protection Regulation) and HIPAA (Health Insurance Portability and Accountability Act).

- **Compliance Requirements:** Depending on your industry and location, you might have specific data compliance requirements regarding data storage location, encryption standards, data access controls, and data retention periods.

Data Governance and Compliance in SharePoint

- **SharePoint Features:** SharePoint offers various features that support data governance and compliance efforts. These include:

    o **Information Rights Management (IRM):** Control access to sensitive documents and restrict copying, printing, or modifying them.

    o **Auditing:** Track user activity and document changes for security and compliance purposes.

    o **eDiscovery:** Facilitate the identification and retrieval of electronic data relevant to legal matters.

    o **Data Loss Prevention (DLP):** Help prevent sensitive data from being accidentally or intentionally shared or leaked.

- **Integration with Azure Information Protection (AIP):** SharePoint integrates with Azure Information Protection (AIP) for a more comprehensive data security and compliance solution. AIP allows you to classify data, apply labels with specific protection policies, and monitor data access across Microsoft cloud services.

Benefits of Effective Data Governance and Compliance

- **Improved Data Security:** Minimize the risk of data breaches and unauthorized access to sensitive information.

- **Enhanced Regulatory Compliance:** Ensure adherence to data privacy laws and regulations to avoid hefty fines and reputational damage.

- **Increased Trust and Transparency:** Demonstrate your commitment to responsible data management practices, fostering trust with stakeholders and customers.

- **Better Data Quality:** Data governance promotes data accuracy, consistency, and completeness, leading to more reliable decision-making.

By implementing a robust data governance strategy and prioritizing data compliance within SharePoint, you can safeguard your organization's information, build trust, and operate within the boundaries set by regulations.

SharePoint and AI

Artificial intelligence (AI) is rapidly transforming various aspects of technology, and SharePoint is no exception. Microsoft is actively integrating AI capabilities into SharePoint, making it a more intelligent and user-friendly platform for collaboration, content management, and knowledge sharing. Here's how AI is shaping the future of SharePoint:

Core AI functionalities in SharePoint:

- **Content Management:**

    o **Automatic Document Classification:** AI can automatically categorize and tag documents based on their content, improving searchability and organization within SharePoint libraries.

    o **Content Enrichment:** AI can extract key information from documents, like dates, names, locations, and summarize content, making it easier for users to find relevant information.

- **Search and Information Retrieval:**

    o **Intelligent Search:** AI-powered search goes beyond keyword matching. It understands the context of user queries and leverages machine learning to deliver more relevant search results, even for phrased queries.

    o **Predictive Search:** As users start typing their search terms, AI can suggest relevant files, documents, or people based on their past search behaviour and activity within SharePoint.

- **User Experience Personalization:**

    o **Content Recommendations:** AI can analyse user activity and recommend content or sites relevant to their work and interests, promoting knowledge discovery within the organization.

    o **Personalized Site Dashboards:** AI can personalize user dashboards by surfacing frequently accessed information and key metrics, allowing users to focus on what matters most to them.

- **Workflow Automation:**
    - **Content Routing:** AI can analyse incoming documents and route them to the appropriate teams or individuals based on content type and pre-defined rules, streamlining workflows.
    - **Task Automation:** AI can automate repetitive tasks such as document approval workflows or data entry, freeing up users' time for more strategic work.

Benefits of AI in SharePoint:

- **Improved User Productivity:** AI features like intelligent search and content recommendations empower users to find information faster and focus on their core tasks.

- **Enhanced Collaboration:** AI-powered features personalize the SharePoint experience, fostering knowledge sharing and better teamwork within the organization.

- **Increased Efficiency:** Automating workflows and tasks with AI streamlines processes and reduces the time spent on manual work.

- **Smarter Content Management:** AI helps organize and categorize information effectively, making it easier to find and manage content within SharePoint.

- **Data-Driven Decisions:** AI-powered analytics can provide valuable insights into user behaviour and content usage, informing data-driven decisions for future improvements.

Overall, AI is transforming SharePoint into a more intelligent and user-centric platform. By leveraging AI capabilities, organizations can empower their employees, streamline collaboration, and unlock the full potential of their information within SharePoint.

Here are some additional points to consider about AI and SharePoint:

- **AI is constantly evolving:** Microsoft is continuously adding new AI functionalities to SharePoint. Stay tuned for future advancements in this space.

- **Security and Compliance:** As AI handles more sensitive data, security and compliance considerations are paramount. Ensure proper safeguards are in place.

- **Human Expertise Remains Crucial:** While AI automates tasks and provides insights, human expertise and decision-making are still essential for optimal results.

By embracing AI in SharePoint, organizations can position themselves for a more productive, collaborative, and knowledge-driven future.

CHAPTER NINE
SHAREPOINT MIGRATION AND INTEGRATION

Planning a SharePoint Migration

A successful SharePoint migration requires careful planning and execution. Here's a roadmap to guide you through the process:

1. Assessment and Planning:

- **Define your goals:** Clearly outline what you want to achieve with the migration. Are you moving to a new SharePoint version, consolidating multiple SharePoint environments, or migrating from a different platform?

- **Inventory your content:** Take stock of everything you have in your existing SharePoint environment. This includes site collections, sites, lists, libraries, files, and metadata.

- **Evaluate content relevance:** Not all content needs to be migrated. Identify outdated, redundant, or irrelevant information that can be archived or deleted.

- **Choose a migration strategy:** There are several migration methods available, each with its advantages and limitations. Consider tools offered by Microsoft, third-party migration solutions, or manual migration for smaller environments.

- **Develop a migration plan:** Create a detailed plan outlining the migration timeline, resources required, tasks involved, and communication strategy for stakeholders.

2. Pre-Migration Preparation:

- **Clean up your data:** Delete or archive outdated or irrelevant information to streamline the migration process and reduce the amount of data to be transferred.

- **Set up your new SharePoint environment:** Configure your new SharePoint environment according to your requirements. This includes creating site collections, defining permissions, and configuring navigation.

- **Test your migration tools:** Before migrating any critical data, thoroughly test your chosen migration tools and processes to identify and troubleshoot any potential issues.

3. Migration Execution:

- **Migrate your content:** Execute the migration process according to your plan. This might involve using migration tools, scripting for complex scenarios, or manual migration for smaller datasets.

- **Monitor and manage the migration:** Closely monitor the migration process for errors or unexpected behaviour. Address any issues promptly to ensure a smooth migration.

4. Post-Migration Activities:

- **Validate and test:** Once the migration is complete, thoroughly test the functionality of your new SharePoint environment. Ensure all content migrated correctly and user permissions are set appropriately.

- **User training and adoption:** Provide adequate training for users on the new SharePoint environment and its functionalities. Encourage user adoption through effective communication and support channels.

- **Ongoing maintenance:** Continuously monitor your new SharePoint environment, address any issues that arise, and implement security updates to ensure optimal performance and data security.

Additional Considerations:

- **Security:** Prioritize data security throughout the migration process. Implement robust security measures in both your source and target SharePoint environments.

- **User Adoption:** A successful migration hinges on user adoption. Develop a communication plan to keep users informed and provide training to ensure they can leverage the new environment effectively.

- **Change Management:** Migration is a change for users. Implement a change management plan to address potential resistance and encourage user buy-in for the new SharePoint environment.

By following these steps and considering the additional factors, you can plan and execute a successful SharePoint migration that minimizes disruption, maximizes user adoption, and unlocks the full potential of your new SharePoint environment.

Integrating SharePoint with Other Systems

Integrating SharePoint with other systems broadens its functionalities and connects it to the wider business ecosystem you rely on. Here's a breakdown of the methods you can leverage to achieve this:

Understanding Integration Methods:

- **Out-of-the-Box Connectors:** SharePoint offers built-in connectors for various popular applications like Microsoft Teams, Power BI, and Dropbox. These connectors enable basic data sharing and synchronization between SharePoint and those applications.

- **Custom API Integration:** For deeper integration beyond pre-built connectors, you can leverage APIs (Application Programming Interfaces) provided by third-party applications. SharePoint's REST API allows you to programmatically interact with data and functionalities of these applications.

- **Third-Party Add-Ins:** The SharePoint Store offers a rich marketplace of third-party add-ins that integrate various applications with SharePoint. These add-ins provide pre-built functionality and often require minimal configuration to set up.

Popular Integration Scenarios:

- **Line-of-Business Systems:** Integrate SharePoint with CRM systems, ERP systems, or other business-critical applications to create a unified platform for data management and collaboration. Streamline processes like lead generation, opportunity management, or project tracking by connecting relevant data between SharePoint and your business systems.

- **Content Management Systems (CMS):** Connect SharePoint with your CMS to streamline document management workflows and ensure consistent content across platforms. For instance, integrate a content approval process within SharePoint before publishing content to your website managed by a CMS.

- **External Data Sources:** Tap into data from external databases or web services using APIs to display relevant information within SharePoint dashboards or reports. You can create insightful reports by integrating sales data from an external CRM or marketing campaign results from a web analytics platform.

- **Productivity Tools:** Enhance collaboration by integrating project management tools, communication platforms, or e-signature services with SharePoint. Integrate project management tools to track tasks and deadlines within SharePoint, or leverage e-signature services for a streamlined document approval process.

Benefits of Third-Party Application Integration:

- **Extended Functionality:** Empower users with a wider range of tools and functionalities within the familiar SharePoint environment.

- **Improved Efficiency:** Streamline workflows by connecting SharePoint with the applications your teams already use. Eliminate the need to switch between different platforms for tasks that can be done collaboratively within SharePoint.

- **Centralized Data Management:** Consolidate information from various sources into a central location for better accessibility and data governance.

- **Enhanced Collaboration:** Foster better teamwork by enabling seamless collaboration across different applications. Break down information silos and ensure everyone has access to the latest data and documents within SharePoint.

Security Considerations:

- **API Permissions:** When using APIs, implement proper access controls to ensure only authorized applications can interact with your SharePoint data. Define granular permissions to grant access only to the specific data needed by the integrated application.

- **Data Security:** Be mindful of the data you expose through integrations and take measures to protect sensitive information. Avoid exposing sensitive data unnecessarily and implement encryption measures if required.

- **Third-Party Vendor Trust:** Choose reputable third-party vendors with a proven track record of security and data privacy practices. Evaluate the security posture of the third-party application before integrating it with SharePoint.

Choosing the Right Integration Approach:

The best method for integrating third-party applications depends on your specific needs and technical expertise:

- **Out-of-the-Box Connectors:** Simple integration needs for popular applications can often be met with built-in connectors, offering a quick and user-friendly solution.

- **Custom API Integration:** For complex integrations or unique requirements, custom development using APIs might be necessary, but it requires programming expertise.

- **Third-Party Add-Ins:** A vast array of pre-built add-ins offer a user-friendly and efficient way to integrate various applications with SharePoint, often with minimal setup. Evaluate the available add-ins in the SharePoint Store to find one that meets your specific needs.

By carefully considering your needs, security, and technical resources, you can leverage third-party application integration to empower your users, streamline workflows, and maximize the value of SharePoint within your organization's ecosystem.

CHAPTER TEN
BEST PRACTICES FOR USING SHAREPOINT

Governance Policies and Procedures

Establishing a well-defined set of governance policies and procedures is essential for ensuring the effective use, security, and organization of your SharePoint environment. Here's a roadmap to guide you through the process:

1. Define Your Goals and Stakeholders:

- **Goals:** Clearly outline what you want to achieve with your SharePoint governance plan. This might include improved information management, streamlined collaboration, enhanced security, or user adoption.

- **Stakeholders:** Identify all parties involved in using and managing SharePoint. This includes end-users, content creators, site owners, administrators, and IT personnel.

2. Develop Core Governance Policies:

- **Information Architecture:** Define the structure and organization of your SharePoint environment. This includes how site collections, sites, content types, and metadata will be used to categorize and manage information.

- **Content Management:** Establish policies for content creation, approval workflows, version control, retention, and disposal of electronic documents and information.

- **Security and Access Controls:** Implement security measures to protect sensitive data. This includes user authentication, authorization levels, encryption practices, and auditing procedures.

- **Backup and Disaster Recovery:** Develop a plan for backing up your SharePoint data and procedures for restoring information in case of emergencies or system failures.

3. Create User-Friendly Procedures:

- **Site Creation and Management:** Establish a clear process for requesting new SharePoint sites, outlining approval procedures, ownership guidelines, and naming conventions.

- **User Training and Support:** Provide user training materials and support channels to help users navigate the SharePoint environment effectively and understand best practices for collaboration and content management.

- **Change Management:** Develop a communication plan to keep users informed about any changes to SharePoint policies, procedures, or functionalities. This helps with user adoption and minimizes disruption.

4. Implement and Maintain Governance:

- **Roles and Responsibilities:** Assign clear roles and responsibilities for SharePoint governance tasks. This might involve designating site owners, content approvers, and IT administrators.

- **Monitoring and Auditing:** Regularly monitor user activity, track content access, and audit changes to ensure adherence to governance policies and identify potential security risks.

- **Continuous Improvement:** Review and update your SharePoint governance policies and procedures periodically to adapt to evolving needs, security threats, and new functionalities within the platform.

Additional Considerations:

- **Alignment with Business Needs:** Ensure your SharePoint governance plan aligns with your organization's overall business objectives and information management strategies.

- **Scalability:** Consider the future growth of your organization and design a governance plan that can scale to accommodate increasing data volumes and user needs.

- **Enforcement:** Establish a clear enforcement mechanism for governance policies. This might involve training managers on their role in enforcing policies or setting up automated processes to identify and address policy violations.

Benefits of Effective SharePoint Governance:

- **Improved Information Management:** Ensures information is organized, secure, and readily accessible to authorized users.

- **Enhanced Collaboration:** Streamlines collaboration processes and fosters a knowledge-sharing culture within the organization.

- **Increased Productivity:** Empowers users to find information faster and work more efficiently.

- **Reduced Risks:** Mitigates security risks and helps ensure compliance with relevant data privacy regulations.

- **Cost Optimization:** Reduces storage costs by eliminating redundant information and streamlining data management practices.

By following these steps and considering the additional factors, you can establish a robust SharePoint governance framework that forms the foundation for a secure, efficient, and user-friendly collaboration platform within your organization.

Performance Optimization

Here's a roadmap to optimize the performance of your SharePoint environment, ensuring a smooth and efficient user experience:

1. Identify Performance Bottlenecks:

- **Monitor User Experience:** Gather feedback from users about slow loading times, unresponsive pages, or other performance issues.

- **Utilize Performance Monitoring Tools:** Leverage built-in SharePoint analytics or third-party monitoring tools to identify areas of inefficiency, pinpoint bottlenecks, and track key performance indicators (KPIs) like page load times and crawl performance.

2. Content Management Strategies:

- **Content Organization:** Structure your content logically using site collections, sites, libraries, and folders. Avoid creating excessively large libraries or nesting folders too deeply.

- **File Size Management:** Implement file size limits for uploaded documents to prevent bloated libraries that strain server resources. Consider alternative storage solutions for very large files.

- **Content Lifecycle Management:** Establish policies for content retention, deletion, and archiving to eliminate redundant or obsolete information that consumes storage space and impacts performance.

3. Search Optimization:

- **Search Indexing:** Fine-tune search indexes to ensure they include the most relevant content and exclude unnecessary data sources. Regularly update search indexes to reflect changes within your SharePoint environment.

- **Crawl Schedule Optimization:** Optimize crawl schedules to balance the need for up-to-date search results with minimizing server load during peak usage times.

4. User Permissions and Security:

- **Review User Permissions:** Regularly review and optimize user permissions to ensure users have only the access level required for their roles. Excessive permissions can strain server resources.

- **External Sharing:** Minimize external sharing of content, especially when large files or folders are involved. Utilize guest access judiciously and consider alternative methods for collaboration with external parties.

5. Database Management:

- **Content Database Sizing:** Monitor the size of your content databases and consider splitting large databases to improve performance. Distribute site collections across multiple databases for optimal load balancing.

- **Search Optimization:** If you utilize a separate search service application, ensure it has sufficient resources allocated to handle search queries efficiently.

6. Hardware and Software Considerations:

- **Hardware Upgrades:** In cases where software optimization reaches its limits, consider upgrading hardware resources like server memory or storage capacity to handle increased workloads.

- **Software Updates:** Keep SharePoint and related software updated with the latest patches and security fixes. Updates often include performance improvements and bug fixes.

7. Additional Techniques:

- **Optimize Page Design:** Minimize the use of complex layouts, excessive images, or unnecessary scripts on SharePoint pages. These elements can slow down page loading times.

- **Content Delivery Networks (CDNs):** Utilize a CDN to cache static content like images or style sheets, reducing the load on your SharePoint server and improving page load times for geographically distributed users.

- **Consider Cloud-Based SharePoint:** If you're using an on-premises SharePoint server, migrating to a cloud-based solution like SharePoint Online can alleviate performance concerns as Microsoft manages the underlying infrastructure.

Remember: Performance optimization is an ongoing process. Regularly monitor your SharePoint environment, identify emerging bottlenecks, and implement suitable optimization techniques to maintain a healthy and responsive platform for your users.

User Training and Adoption Strategies

Achieving successful user adoption is paramount for maximizing the value of your SharePoint environment. Here's a roadmap to guide you in developing effective user training and adoption strategies:

1. Understand Your Users:

- **Identify Needs:** Conduct surveys or focus groups to understand your users' current challenges and pain points related to information management and collaboration.

- **Learning Styles:** Consider the diverse learning styles within your user base. Offer a variety of training materials and formats to cater to different preferences, including video tutorials, written guides, or in-person workshops.

2. Develop Engaging Training Content:

- **Focus on Benefits:** Frame your training around the benefits users will gain by adopting SharePoint. Show them how it can save them time, improve collaboration, or streamline workflows.

- **Actionable Skills:** Focus on teaching users practical skills they can immediately apply in their daily work. Move beyond theoretical concepts and provide step-by-step instructions for common tasks.

- **Bite-Sized Learning:** Break down complex functionalities into smaller, more manageable learning modules. This makes information easier to digest and retain.

3. Delivery Methods and User Support:

- **Variety is Key:** Utilize a mix of training delivery methods like online tutorials, instructor-led workshops, or on-demand video resources to cater to different learning styles and preferences.

- **Just-in-Time Support:** Provide easily accessible support resources like quick reference guides, cheat sheets, or context-sensitive help within the SharePoint environment itself.

- **Empower Super Users:** Identify and train champions within your organization who can provide ongoing peer-to-peer support to their colleagues.

4. Promote User Adoption:

- **Communication is Key:** Keep users informed about the launch of SharePoint, its functionalities, and the benefits it offers. Utilize multiple communication channels like emails, newsletters, or internal communication platforms.

- **Incentivize Usage:** Consider gamification or recognition programs to encourage users to explore and actively utilize SharePoint functionalities in their daily work.

- **Success Stories:** Showcase real-world examples of how other teams or departments are successfully leveraging SharePoint to achieve better results.

5. Continuous Improvement:

- **Gather Feedback:** Regularly solicit feedback from users to understand their experience with SharePoint and identify areas for improvement in training materials or support resources.

- **Adapting to Change:** As SharePoint evolves with new features and functionalities, keep your training content and support resources updated to ensure users stay informed and proficient.

Additional Tips:

- **Executive Sponsorship:** Gain buy-in from leadership to emphasize the importance of SharePoint adoption within the organization.

- **Change Management:** Address potential resistance to change through effective communication and training. Highlight how SharePoint can improve workflows and empower users, not replace existing practices.

- **Focus on User Experience:** Prioritize user experience by ensuring SharePoint is intuitive and easy to navigate. Regularly review user feedback and make adjustments to optimize the user interface for a smooth experience.

By following these strategies and remaining attentive to user needs, you can develop a comprehensive user training and adoption program that sets your organization on the path to successful SharePoint utilization. Remember, user adoption is an ongoing process. Continuously monitor progress, adapt your approach based on feedback, and celebrate successes to keep users engaged and maximize the value of SharePoint within your organization.

<u>Troubleshooting Common Issues</u>
Sure, here are some common troubleshooting tips for SharePoint:

General Issues:

- **Unable to access SharePoint:**
    - **Check internet connectivity:** Ensure a stable internet connection for both your device and the SharePoint server.
    - **Verify login credentials:** Double-check your username and password for typos or try resetting your password if forgotten.

- o **Check browser compatibility:** Make sure you are using a supported web browser by Microsoft for optimal SharePoint functionality. Popular options include Chrome, Firefox, and Edge.

- o **Clear browser cache:** Clear your browser's cache and cookies to eliminate potential conflicts with stored data.

- **Slow loading times:**

  - o **Optimize your content:** Reduce the size of uploaded files, avoid complex page layouts with excessive images, and minimize unnecessary scripts.

  - o **Consider a CDN:** Implement a Content Delivery Network (CDN) to cache static content and improve page load times for geographically distributed users.

  - o **Review server load:** If you manage an on-premises SharePoint server, ensure it has sufficient hardware resources (CPU, memory) to handle user traffic.

- **Search functionality issues:**

  - o **Refine your search query:** Use clear and concise keywords, and leverage search filters to narrow down results.

  - o **Review search indexes:** Ensure search indexes are up-to-date and include the relevant content sources you expect to find through searches.

  - o **Contact administrator:** If search functionality is persistently problematic, contact your SharePoint administrator for further troubleshooting.

Synchronization Issues (SharePoint Online and OneDrive):

- **Sync errors:**

  - o **Check internet connectivity:** Verify a stable internet connection for successful data synchronization.

  - o **Restart devices:** Sometimes a simple restart of your computer or mobile device can resolve temporary glitches with the synchronization process.

  - o **Free up storage space:** Ensure sufficient storage space on your device to accommodate downloaded SharePoint content.

  - o **Unlink and relink OneDrive:** In case of persistent errors, try unlinking your OneDrive account from SharePoint and then relinking it to establish a fresh connection.

- **Files not syncing:**

  - **Check file types and sizes:** Be aware of any limitations on file types or sizes that SharePoint or OneDrive may have for synchronization.

  - **Check file permissions:** Ensure you have the necessary permissions to access and synchronize the files or folders you're trying to sync.

Security and Permissions Issues:

- **Access denied errors:**

  - **Verify user permissions:** Confirm that you have the appropriate permissions assigned to access the specific SharePoint site, list, or document you're trying to access.

  - **Contact site owner:** If you believe you should have access, reach out to the site owner or SharePoint administrator to request the necessary permissions.

- **Unexpected behaviour:**

  - **Clear browser cache:** Clearing your browser cache can sometimes resolve unexpected behaviour caused by outdated cached data.

  - **Try a different browser:** If the issue persists in one browser, test using a different web browser to isolate the problem.

Remember: These are general troubleshooting tips. If you encounter specific error messages or experience issues beyond these basic steps, it's recommended to consult official Microsoft documentation or seek help from your SharePoint administrator for more in-depth troubleshooting assistance.

CHAPTER ELEVEN
FUTURE TRENDS IN SHAREPOINT

Evolution of SharePoint in the Cloud

The move to the cloud has been a defining shift for SharePoint, transforming it from a primarily on-premises document management system into a robust collaboration platform. Here's a closer look at the evolution of SharePoint in the cloud:

Early Days: On-Premises Dominance (Pre-2013):

- **Limited Collaboration Features:** Early versions of SharePoint focused on document management, with rudimentary collaboration features.

- **Version Control and Offline Access:** Offered basic functionalities like version control and offline access for documents.

- **Complex Administration:** Setting up and maintaining on-premises SharePoint servers required significant IT expertise.

The Cloud Revolution and Rise of SharePoint Online (2013 - Present):

- **SharePoint 2013 - Embracing the Cloud:** The introduction of SharePoint 2013 marked a turning point, offering a cloud-based version alongside the on-premises option. This provided greater accessibility and scalability.

- **Improved Mobile Experiences:** SharePoint Online prioritized mobile responsiveness, allowing users to access and collaborate on documents from anywhere on various devices.

- **Seamless Integration with Microsoft 365:** SharePoint became a core component of Microsoft 365, integrating seamlessly with Teams, OneDrive, and other productivity applications. This fostered a unified platform for communication, collaboration, and content management.

Key Benefits of SharePoint Online:

- **Reduced IT Burden:** Microsoft manages the underlying infrastructure, freeing IT teams to focus on strategic initiatives.

- **Automatic Updates:** Regular updates and security patches are automatically applied, ensuring users have access to the latest features and improved security.

- **Scalability and Cost-Effectiveness:** Cloud-based SharePoint scales effortlessly to accommodate growing organizations and data volumes, often with predictable subscription costs.

- **Enhanced Collaboration:** Integration with Microsoft 365 applications streamlines workflows and facilitates better teamwork across departments and locations.

- **Advanced Features:** SharePoint Online offers a wider range of functionalities compared to on-premises versions, including AI-powered search, content recommendations, and workflow automation.

The Future of SharePoint in the Cloud:

- **AI Integration:** Expect deeper integration of AI for more intelligent content management, personalized user experiences, and automated tasks.

- **Focus on Security and Compliance:** As data privacy regulations evolve, SharePoint Online will continue to prioritize robust security features and compliance capabilities.

- **The Low-Code/No-Code Revolution:** Empowering users with low-code/no-code tools for building custom workflows and applications within SharePoint will be a growing trend.

- **Hybrid Deployments:** Many organizations will likely adopt hybrid deployments, combining on-premises SharePoint with SharePoint Online for a tailored solution that meets their specific needs.

Overall, the evolution of SharePoint in the cloud has transformed it into a dynamic collaboration platform that empowers users, simplifies IT management, and fosters a more connected and productive work environment.

Impact of AI and Machine Learning

Artificial intelligence (AI) and machine learning (ML) are significantly impacting SharePoint, transforming it from a content management system into an intelligent platform that anticipates user needs and streamlines collaboration processes. Here's a breakdown of the key areas where AI and ML are making a difference:

Enhanced Content Management:

- **Automatic Document Classification:** AI can automatically categorize and tag documents based on their content, making them easier to find and organize within SharePoint libraries. This eliminates manual tagging and ensures consistency in information architecture.

- **Content Enrichment:** AI can extract key information from documents, like names, dates, locations, and summarize content. This enriches search results and allows users to quickly grasp the gist of a document without having to open it.

- **Intelligent Search:** AI goes beyond keyword matching in search queries. It understands the context of user intent and leverages machine learning to deliver more relevant search results, even for phrased or natural language queries.

- **Predictive Search:** As users start typing their search terms, AI can suggest relevant files, documents, or people based on their past search behaviour and activity within SharePoint. This saves time and effort in finding the information they need.

Improved User Experience:

- **Content Recommendations:** AI can analyse user activity and recommend content or sites relevant to their work and interests. This fosters knowledge discovery within the organization and helps users stay abreast of important information.

- **Personalized Dashboards:** AI can personalize user dashboards by surfacing frequently accessed information and key metrics. This allows users to focus on what matters most to them and reduces information overload.

Workflow Automation:

- **Content Routing:** AI can analyse incoming documents and route them to the appropriate teams or individuals based on content type and pre-defined rules. This streamlines workflows and eliminates manual sorting of documents.

- **Task Automation:** AI can automate repetitive tasks such as document approval workflows or data entry. This frees up users' time for more strategic work and reduces the risk of human error.

Additional Benefits:

- **Improved Security:** AI can be used to detect and prevent security threats, such as malware or phishing attempts, within SharePoint.

- **Data-Driven Insights:** AI-powered analytics can provide valuable insights into user behaviour and content usage, informing data-driven decisions for future improvements to the platform and content management strategies.

Overall, AI and machine learning are transforming SharePoint into a more intelligent and user-centric platform. By leveraging these capabilities, organizations can empower their employees, streamline collaboration, unlock the full potential of their information within SharePoint, and make data-driven decisions for continuous improvement.

Here are some additional points to consider:

- **AI is constantly evolving:** Microsoft is continuously adding new AI functionalities to SharePoint. Stay tuned for future advancements in intelligent content management and personalized user experiences.

- **Human Expertise Remains Crucial:** While AI automates tasks and provides insights, human expertise and decision-making are still essential for optimal results. AI should be seen as a tool to augment human capabilities.

- **Security and Compliance:** As AI handles more sensitive data, security and compliance considerations are paramount. Ensure proper safeguards are in place to protect sensitive information.

By embracing AI and machine learning in SharePoint, organizations can position themselves for a more productive, collaborative, and knowledge-driven future.

Emerging Features and Innovations

SharePoint is constantly evolving, with Microsoft actively integrating new features and functionalities to enhance user experience, improve collaboration, and leverage cutting-edge technologies like AI and machine learning. Here's a glimpse into some emerging trends and innovations shaping the future of SharePoint:

1. Deeper Integration with Microsoft 365 Apps:

- **Co-authoring across Applications:** Seamless co-authoring will extend beyond SharePoint pages to documents within OneDrive and other Microsoft 365 applications. This will allow real-time collaboration on various content types, fostering a more unified workspace experience.

- **Composite Applications within SharePoint Pages:** Imagine embedding interactive Power Apps or canvas apps directly within SharePoint pages. This empowers users to create custom functionalities without needing to switch between applications.

2. Enhanced Mobile Experience:

- **Improved Offline Functionality:** Expect richer offline capabilities, allowing users to work on SharePoint documents and tasks even without an internet connection. This will significantly improve productivity on the go.

- **Voice Commands and Mobile-Specific Features:** Voice commands for searching content or interacting with SharePoint functionalities might become more prevalent. Additionally, expect features specifically designed for the mobile interface to optimize the user experience on smartphones and tablets.

3. Artificial Intelligence for an Intelligent Workplace:

- **Advanced Content Understanding:** AI will go beyond simple document classification. It will analyse content to extract insights, identify relationships between documents, and suggest connections or relevant information to users.

- **Smarter Search and Information Retrieval:** AI-powered search will become even more intuitive, understanding the context and intent behind user queries to deliver highly relevant results. Imagine natural language search capabilities that mimic how humans ask questions.

4. Focus on Low-Code/No-Code Customization:

- **Empowering Users as Citizen Developers:** Expect tools that allow users with minimal coding experience to build custom workflows, automate tasks, and personalize their SharePoint experience. This will democratize application development and empower business users to solve problems without relying heavily on IT teams.

5. Evolving Security and Compliance Landscape:

- **Data Loss Prevention (DLP) and Information Protection:** As data privacy regulations become more stringent, expect robust DLP features within SharePoint to prevent sensitive information leaks. Additionally, functionalities for better information lifecycle management and data classification will be crucial.

- **Zero Trust Security Model:** A growing focus on zero-trust security principles will likely influence SharePoint's security architecture. This means continuous verification and authorization checks regardless of a user's location or device.

Overall, these emerging features and innovations highlight Microsoft's commitment to transforming SharePoint into a dynamic platform that caters to the evolving needs of modern workplaces. By embracing AI, low-code customization, and a focus on user experience, SharePoint is poised to empower teamwork, streamline workflows, and unlock the true potential of information within your organization.

CHAPTER TWELVE
RESOURCES AND REFERENCES

Official Documentation

For the most accurate and up-to-date information on SharePoint, it's recommended to refer directly to Microsoft's official documentation. Here's how to find it:

1. **Microsoft Learn:** This is the primary resource for official SharePoint documentation. It offers a comprehensive collection of learning modules, step-by-step guides, API references, and more. You can find it by searching for "[SharePoint documentation Microsoft Learn]" (without the brackets) in your web browser.

2. **Microsoft 365 Documentation:** SharePoint Online documentation is also integrated within the broader Microsoft 365 documentation. This site offers various resources relevant to SharePoint Online and its integration with other Microsoft 365 applications. Search for "[Microsoft 365 documentation]" (without the brackets) to access it.

3. **Specific Product Documentation:** When searching for functionalities within a specific SharePoint version (e.g., SharePoint Server 2019), include the version number in your search queries along with "Microsoft documentation" to ensure you're accessing the most relevant content.

Key Topics Covered in Official Documentation:

- Getting started with SharePoint (user guides, tutorials)

- Managing and customizing SharePoint sites and libraries

- Working with content (uploading, editing, collaboration features)

- Security and permissions management

- Integrating SharePoint with other applications

- Troubleshooting common issues

- Developer resources (API references, code samples)

By utilizing these official documentation resources, you can be confident you have the latest information for all your SharePoint needs.

Additional Tips:

- **Search Functionality:** Both Microsoft Learn and Microsoft 365 documentation offer robust search functionalities. Utilize relevant keywords to find the specific information you're looking for.

- **Version Specific Information:** Pay attention to any versioning information within the documentation to ensure it applies to the particular version of SharePoint you're using.

- **Stay Updated:** Microsoft frequently updates its documentation. Consider subscribing to updates or checking back periodically to stay informed about new features and functionalities.

I hope this refined response provides you with the best possible guidance for finding official SharePoint documentation!

Community and Support Forums

Beyond official documentation, a vibrant community of SharePoint users and administrators exists online, offering valuable support and insights. Here are some popular forums where you can connect with peers, find solutions, and stay informed about SharePoint:

1. Microsoft Tech Community:

- **Official Microsoft Platform:** This is an excellent starting point for finding community-driven discussions and support resources directly hosted by Microsoft.

- **Specific SharePoint Groups:** Search for "SharePoint" within the Tech Community to find dedicated groups for various SharePoint versions (Online, Server), functionalities, and specific challenges.

- **Ask Questions and Share Knowledge:** Engage with other users, post questions about issues you're facing, or share your own knowledge and solutions to help others within the community.

2. Spiceworks Community:

- **IT Professional Network:** Spiceworks caters to a broad IT professional audience, with a dedicated section for SharePoint discussions.

- **Real-World Scenarios:** Spiceworks discussions often focus on real-world scenarios and troubleshooting challenges faced by IT professionals managing SharePoint environments.

- **Search Functionality:** Utilize the search bar to find discussions relevant to your specific SharePoint query.

3. TechRepublic Forums:

- **Technology News and Community:** TechRepublic offers a forum section alongside its technology news and articles.

- **SharePoint Discussions:** While not as extensive as other options, you might find relevant discussions about SharePoint functionalities, best practices, and user experiences.

- **Search Functionality:** Utilize the search bar to find discussions relevant to your specific SharePoint query.

4. Reddit:

- **Subreddit for SharePoint:** The subreddit r/SharePoint offers a platform for discussions, news updates, and resource sharing related to the platform.

- **Wide Range of Topics:** Discussions on Reddit can cover a wide range of topics, from general SharePoint questions to specific functionalities and troubleshooting.

- **Up-to-date Information:** The active nature of Reddit helps keep discussions and information somewhat up-to-date.

Additional Tips for Utilizing Community Forums:

- **Search Before Posting:** Before creating a new thread, search the forum archives to see if your question has already been addressed.

- **Provide Context:** When asking a question, provide clear details about your specific situation, SharePoint version, and any error messages you're encountering. The more context you offer, the better the assistance you'll receive.

- **Be Respectful and Professional:** Maintain a professional and respectful tone in your interactions within the forums.

- **Share Your Knowledge:** If you have expertise in a particular area, consider helping others by answering questions and sharing your knowledge within the community.

Remember, community forums are a valuable resource for learning, troubleshooting, and staying informed about SharePoint. Utilize them effectively to complement the knowledge gained from official documentation and enhance your overall SharePoint experience.

CHAPTER THIRTEEN
INTRODUCTION TO MICROSOFT SHAREPOINT

Common Terminology

Sure, here's a rundown of some common terminology you'll encounter in SharePoint:

Sites and Content Organization:

- **Site Collection:** A group of SharePoint sites that share the same administration settings, security model, and often a common theme.

- **Site:** A collaborative workspace within a SharePoint collection, typically focused on a specific team, department, or project. Think of it as a container for your content.

- **Subsite:** A website nested underneath a parent site within a SharePoint collection. It inherits permissions and some configurations from the parent site but can have its own unique features and functionalities.

- **List:** A structured collection of data items displayed in rows and columns, similar to a spreadsheet. Lists are ideal for managing tasks, tracking information, or building custom workflows.

- **Library:** A central location for storing, managing, and sharing various types of files and documents within a SharePoint site. Common examples include document libraries, picture libraries, and video libraries.

- **Folder:** A way to categorize and organize items within a SharePoint list or library. Folders help maintain a clutter-free environment and improve information findability.

Content Management and Collaboration:

- **Version Control:** The ability to track changes made to documents over time, allowing you to revert to previous versions if needed.

- **Checkout/Check-in:** A mechanism for controlling who can edit a document at a specific time. Checking out a document prevents others from making changes while you're working on it.

- **Metadata:** Additional descriptive information attached to documents or list items, making them easier to find and categorize. Examples include author name, department, keywords, or due dates.

- **Workflow:** An automated sequence of actions or tasks triggered by specific events within SharePoint. Workflows can streamline approvals, automate notifications, or manage document lifecycles.

- **Permissions:** Control access to SharePoint sites, lists, libraries, and items. Permissions determine who can view, edit, or contribute content within SharePoint.

Search and Navigation:

- **View:** A specific way to display information within a SharePoint list or library. Common views include All Items, Calendar view, or Kanban board view, depending on the list type and functionalities.

- **Search:** The functionality within SharePoint to find specific content using keywords or filters. Advanced search options allow for more refined searches based on metadata or other criteria.

- **Navigation:** The way users find their way around a SharePoint site or collection. Navigation elements include menus, breadcrumbs, and quick launch bars that provide easy access to frequently used content.

Additional Terms:

- **Web Part:** Reusable components that add specific functionalities to SharePoint pages. Examples include calendars, document lists, or custom forms.

- **Content Type:** A reusable definition that specifies the type of information allowed within a SharePoint list or library column. It dictates what kind of data can be entered (text, date, number) and how it should be displayed.

- **Site Owner:** The user with the highest level of permissions for a SharePoint site. Site owners can manage settings, configure security, and add or remove users.

By understanding this common SharePoint terminology, you'll be well on your way to navigating the platform effectively and collaborating seamlessly with your colleagues.

Acronyms and Abbreviations
General SharePoint Acronyms:

- **SP** - SharePoint

- **SPO** - SharePoint Online (the cloud-based version)

- **SPS** - SharePoint Server (the on-premises version)

- **CDN** - Content Delivery Network

- **UI** - User Interface

- **UX** - User Experience

- **API** - Application Programming Interface

Acronyms Related to Sites and Content Management:

- **SC** - Site Collection

- **Subsite** - A website nested under a parent site within a collection

- **List** - A structured collection of data items in rows and columns

- **Library** - A central location for storing and managing files and documents

- **WCM** - Web Content Management

Collaboration and Workflow Acronyms:

- **SSO** - Single Sign-On

- **RBAC** - Role-Based Access Control

- **BPM** - Business Process Management

- **OOTB** - Out-of-the-Box (pre-built functionalities)

Search and Navigation Acronyms:

- **CAML** - Collaborative Applications Markup Language (used for queries)

- **KB** - Knowledge Base

Additional SharePoint Acronyms:

- **GA** - Generally Available (released version)

MVP - Most Valuable Professional (Microsoft program for SharePoint experts)

THANK YOU FOR READING